Keys
to
the
Classroom

Keys
to
the
Classroom

A Teacher's Guide
to the First Month of School

Carrol Moran
Judy Stobbe
Wendy Baron
Janette Miller
Ellen Moir

CORWIN PRESS, INC.
A Sage Publications Company
Newbury Park, California

For information address:

Corwin Press, Inc.
A Sage Publications Company
2455 Teller Road
Newbury Park, California 91320

SAGE Publications Ltd.
6 Bonhill Street
London EC2A 4PU
United Kingdom

SAGE Publications India Pvt. Ltd.
M-32 Market
Greater Kailash I
New Delhi 110 048 India

Printed in the United States of America

Library of Congress Cataloging-in-Publication Data

Main entry under title:

Keys to the classroom: a teacher's guide to the first month of school
    / Carrol Moran . . . [et al.].
        p.   cm.
    Includes bibliographical references (p.   ).
    ISBN 0-8039-6014-X
    1. Teaching.
    LB1025.3.K49 1992
    371.1′02—dc20   91-36935
                                                                                        CIP

96 10 9 8 7 6 5 4

Corwin Press Production Editor: Tara S. Mead

Contents

Acknowledgments

We would like to thank the 43 new teachers we worked with in the Santa Cruz County New Teacher Project for providing the impetus for this guide. They shared freely the challenges and frustrations that most teachers face on entering the profession. They showed us very clearly how crucial the first month is in setting the standards of interaction for the rest of the year.

We would also like to thank the following contributors, reviewers, and critics for all of their valuable input: Marina Cook, Susana Dutro, Pola Espinoza, Liz Gordon, Kathy Idoine, Teri Marchese, Alison Woolpert, and Marney Cox.

In addition, we would also like to thank our typists, Shirlene Campbell, Millie Ashley, and Alice Misumi; our translator, Luz María S. Steves; and our graphics artist, Carrie Wilker, for the wonderful work they have done.

It is our hope in creating this guide that we can ease new teachers' entry into classroom teaching. We want to take the mystery out of the first month, and we have tried to spell out clearly the many keys used by experienced teachers to open the school year successfully.

CARROL MORAN
JUDY STOBBE
WENDY BARON
JANETTE MILLER
ELLEN MOIR

About the Authors

Wendy Baron, in her 17 years as an educator, has taught grades K-6, served as a Chapter I Reading and Perceptual Motor Specialist, and has been a natural science teacher. She has also worked at the University of California, Santa Cruz, supervising and instructing prospective teachers. She currently works with the Santa Cruz County New Teacher Project, advising and coaching novice teachers and coordinating a staff development program for second-year teachers. She has a B.A. in psychology, an M.A. in curriculum and instruction, and an administrative services credential. She has provided numerous workshops to educators on such topics as whole language, the writing process, authentic assessment, use of math manipulatives, teaching strategies, communication and conflict resolution, thematic planning, peer coaching, and new teacher induction.

Janette Miller has extensive training in classroom management, peer coaching, and evaluation. She is a fellow of the Central California Writers' Project and the Monterey Bay Area Math Project. She has particularly enjoyed training novice and veteran teachers in classroom management techniques, direct teaching model, the reading/writing connection, and experiential math strategies. She has been a classroom teacher, a reading specialist, an adviser for the California New Teacher Project, and peer evaluator for new employees in the Santa Cruz City Schools District. She is currently teaching third grade at Westlake School in Santa Cruz.

Ellen Moir has been a Supervisor of Teacher Education at the University of California at Santa Cruz since 1979, where she teaches bilingual method courses and oversees the student teaching program. She is also the Director of the UCSC-led New Teacher Project, which has received grants of more than $800,000 over the last three years from the California Department of Education and the Commission for Teacher Credentialing to Support Beginning Teachers. She is the director of two video documentaries: *Passage into Teaching* (1990) and *Bilingual Education: An Inside View* (1984). In addition, she is the author of several publications on teacher training and in-service education and has served as a consultant to school districts throughout California.

Carrol Moran is an educational consultant specializing in bilingual education and second-language literacy. She has worked in education for 20 years, teaching preschool through college levels. During her 14 years with the Pajaro Valley School District, she worked as a classroom teacher, reading specialist, language specialist, and resource and mentor teacher. She has written extensive curriculum in social studies, literature-based reading, English as a second language, and math. She is the author of several publications, including *The Bridge: Spanish to English*, a guide to teaching literacy in a bilingual setting; *A Novel Idea*, a guide to teaching literature-based reading; and *Colors of the Earthquake*, a children's book about the Loma Prieta quake, illustrated by children. She also writes curriculum for students acquiring English for several major publishing companies. Currently, she is a doctoral student at Stanford and does educational consulting across the nation.

Judy Stobbe has been an innovative educational leader in Santa Cruz County and around the United States since 1972. She is a sought-after consultant and teacher trainer in the areas of emergent literacy, early childhood math instruction, second-language acquisition, and bilingual education. She has worked in the Teacher Education Department at the University of California, Santa Cruz, where she taught methodology courses as well as supervised bilingual student teachers. As an adviser for the Santa Cruz County New Teacher Project, she worked with new bilingual teachers as a mentor and coach. Out of this experience came the precursor to the present volume, *The Keys . . . Entering the Classroom*, which provided much-needed insight into the secrets of a successful classroom. She is an active participant in many professional organizations, including the California Association for Bilingual Education and Phi Delta Kappa. Currently she divides her time between teaching in a bilingual kindergarten, in order to keep her hand in the reality of classroom teaching, and working as a free-lance writer for major publishing companies.

Introduction

The purpose of this guide is to pass on to new teachers the keys to opening the school year successfully. During that first month, as in the beginning of a journey, anything and everything are possible. Some spontaneous journeys just happen and turn out great. Some, however, can be very arduous, stressful, and exhausting. Having a few keys to open vehicles and unlock doors can make a journey easier and can allow you to spend more time getting to know people. The same is true for the beginning of school. We have tried to think through all the necessary preparations and planning activities that will foster cooperation and a sense of belonging in the group as well as present you with a great many opportunities to learn about your students. Use the keys offered here to make your trip smoother, but remember, you are in charge of the trip. Consider this as your *Michelin Guide* to the first month of school. Take the suggestions you like, use the activities that fit your style, and integrate them with your own vision of what you want your class to be.

The following are the basic principles that have guided the development of this curriculum:

(1) Your students will benefit from an organized, stimulating physical environment that they have participated in creating.

(2) Students will feel more comfortable knowing what to expect in established daily routines.

(3) Students will learn a great deal from each other in cooperative and interactive activities when provided with a variety of learning situations.

(4) Effective literacy development is based on reading excellent literature and writing from one's own voice.

(5) Math concepts that are presented developmentally with manipulatives and conceptual understanding preceding paper-and-pencil work will stimulate thought processes as well as enhance computation skills.

(6) Assessment of students is an ongoing daily activity of observation and documentation of student learning.

(7) Content should be integrated throughout subject areas.

(8) During the first month, content must take a backseat to the development of a sense of group and the learning of expectations, routines, and procedures.

The primary objectives for teachers in the first month of school are as follows:

- to build a sense of inclusion with students
- to establish the routines and procedures of the classroom
- to learn students' strengths and needs
- to set the tone of a love for learning

This curriculum is designed to help you meet these objectives.

Many veteran teachers have started their preparation for the first day of school by using the earlier version of this volume, *The Keys . . . Entering the Classroom*. First-year teachers have been known to keep it on their bedside tables, for nightly reading. We believe you will find this revised and expanded version just as indispensable. Chapter 1, "Creating the Environment," and Chapter 2, "Daily Routines and Procedures," are designed to help you think through the details that can make or break your daily routine. Chapter 3, "The First Day of School . . . A Detailed Account," takes you minute by minute through the day. It will put to rest any fears you have that you will never be able to keep those kids busy all day.

Chapter 4, "Activities for the First Month," describes tried-and-true activities that can be the core of your cooperative program or a safety net to fall back on when your plans have gone awry. All student worksheets are provided in English and Spanish. The material in Chapter 5, "Fingerplays and Songs for Oral Language," will provide the K-3 teacher with not only excellent language development, but also a positive transition activity that cuts down on discipline problems.

Chapter 6, "Assessment of Students," contains state-of-the-art suggestions for classroom-based assessment that can be the beginning of student portfolios and will provide you with the information you need to plan appropriate lessons. Chapter 7, "Parent Communications," contains model letters to parents in English and Spanish—an incredible time-saver for teachers in bilingual classrooms. The final chapter, "Resources," provides suggestions for reading for your own professional development as well as appropriate read-alouds for each grade level in English and Spanish.

1 Creating the Environment

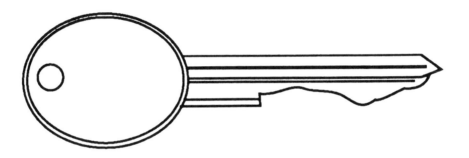

Organize your classroom in a way that allows for a variety of learning styles and situations, and that keeps materials organized and accessible to students.

CHAPTER CONTENTS

ROOM ARRANGEMENT

Environment plays a critical role in the classroom. How you set up the classroom will affect what goes on there. Before the students arrive on the first day, you will want to organize your classroom carefully. The following are suggestions for activity areas you may want to plan for. Note that your space, furniture, and equipment may not allow you to set all these up as separate areas, but you will want to consider where the activities might take place given your particular limitations.

- a space for whole-group meeting on the floor (rug area) near the bulletin board for the calendar and a chalkboard
- student seating to promote cooperation and communication (e.g., table groupings or desk clusters)
- a table large enough for a group of eight students, to be used for teacher-directed small-group work (If you have an aide who works with groups, you will need two tables.)
- an art area including easels, paint supplies, yarn, glue for projects, construction paper, and so on
- a listening center for two to four students at a small table or even a floor space equipped with a tape recorder, two to four sets of earphones, a jack to hook up the earphones to the tape recorder, and a record player
- center areas for two to four students (e.g., small tables or individual desks to use for independent activities arranged around the periphery of the room)
- a library corner with books displayed so students can see covers (with space for student-produced class books and a space to read)
- an observation area for things you or your students bring in (e.g., shells displayed in a sea-life theme or objects that have odors displayed in a five-senses theme)

For kindergarten and possibly first grade, you will need these areas as well:

- a dramatic play area, including playhouse furniture, dolls, phone, dress-up clothes, and the like (can be changed during the year to a post office, grocery store, or another type of place)
- a construction area for blocks, Legos, and other manipulatives

You need not have each area up and running the first day of school, but planning for an area will allow you to enrich the classroom with materials and not have to rearrange furniture to create the space. (Note: Be sure to establish noisy and quiet areas in proper proximity—playhouse, blocks, projects, and art in the noisy part of the room; listening center and library corner in the quiet part of the room.)

Keys to the Classroom. © 1992 Corwin Press, Inc.

Seating

Seating will depend on your preference. In general, kindergartners do not need assigned seats but will need cubbies or mailboxes. Have cubbies labeled with names the first day.

First and second graders may use tables or desks. If tables are used, students will need cubbies. Usually first and second graders have assigned seats for part of the day, but the arrangement allows for their seats to be used in different ways at different times (e.g., for reading groups or centers).

You may want to assign seats to intermediate-level students based on boy-girl or alphabetical order. This seating arrangement can be temporary; as you get to know students' behaviors and abilities, you can make appropriate changes.

Organization of Supplies

Environment includes more than just the arrangement of furniture. You also want to give careful consideration to material storage, including everyday supplies (crayons, paste, scissors, paper, and the like) as well as games, puzzles, blocks, books, and so on.

For general supplies it is useful to color code or symbol code your room to assist students in being independent when cleaning up. Storing items in tubs or boxes that are labeled with a geometric shape that corresponds to a shape on the shelf where the item is stored is an easy way to organize material storage. For example, if you have five tables or five groups of desks, label each with a piece of construction paper covered with clear Con-Tact paper as follows: orange rectangle, red circle, green triangle, yellow square, blue oval. Then label five supply tubs (containing paste, scissors, crayons, and so on) and the shelf where each tub is stored with the corresponding shapes/colors. Now your students can easily find and return the supplies they need to use.

Other items that the students use on a regular basis (e.g., puzzles, math manipulatives, games, Legos) can be stored in a consistent place on a shelf by labeling the box/tub with a shape or color that corresponds to a color on the shelf. These items may not necessarily always be used at one table, so these shapes need not correspond to the table shapes.

Decisions to Make

Will individual students have their own crayons, pencils, scissors, and so on? We suggest that they don't. Instead, organize one tub/group with all the supplies the group will need. The tubs could be labeled with the group name or with your color-coding system. It then becomes the group's responsibility to maintain it.

If your students have individual desks, you might consider having individual supplies. If you do, however, be sure to provide each student with a container in which to keep the supplies—a Ziploc bag, a box to be kept on top of the desk, or the like.

Be sure to have a designated place for extra supplies or where found items can be placed. For example, provide a place where a student can find a pencil if the one from his or her own supplies is missing. (Do not put new pencils in this extra supply.)

Who will be responsible for getting supplies, if they are not individually housed? A supplies monitor, a team captain, you? This may vary from activity to activity, but the clear answer is that it should not be you.

To facilitate getting books and materials back at the end of the year, number the items before you distribute them to students and record the information in your plan book.

ENVIRONMENT CHECKLIST

In my classroom:

✔ Many types of books, both fiction and nonfiction and various genres, are available for browsing and reading.

✔ A library corner is provided.

✔ Children have access to tapes and records that accompany books.

✔ Reading material other than books is provided.

✔ Films and filmstrips are available.

✔ Creative materials are available for personal interpretation.

✔ Research opportunities are provided.

✔ Space is allocated for oral activities (readers' theater, choral speaking, playacting) so as not to interfere with silent reading or listening activities.

✔ Tapes are provided so that students may listen to their own stories or their oral reading experiences.

✔ A quiet corner is established where students may write, read, dream, think.

✔ Bulletin boards display student work, allow for learning and interaction, and support what is being taught.

✔ Displays stimulate interest in reading.

✔ The space is neat and organized efficiently.

✔ The room provides opportunities for students to make choices from several activities, places to work, and so on.

PREPARATION PRIOR TO THE FIRST DAY

The following pages outline some things you may want to have prepared before the students arrive.

K-6: A class list. A list that includes all students' addresses, bus numbers, and telephone numbers is a must. Add new students to your list immediately. You should either look at a map or take a tour of your attendance area, so you are familiar with the neighborhoods. See your school secretary to find out this information.

It is easier in the long run to make your own class list in alphabetical order by first name. You will usually look for students by their first names, and using the school-provided list, which is in alphabetical order by last name, slows you down.

Establish a handy place to keep this list (e.g., you might put it on a clipboard and hang it near your desk). You will be referring to it often throughout the year, but especially during the first month of school. Make several copies and use them as checklists for the return of free-lunch forms and so on.

K-2: Name tags. Make each student a name tag that includes first and last name, address, bus number, and the number of your classroom. Have extra blank name tags on hand for unexpected students. It is helpful to make these tags out of sturdy material—even laminated—and form them into necklaces with yarn so they can be used for the first couple of weeks of school. Consider coding the name tags in some way—perhaps using different-colored roving (yarn) or different shapes— for groups of six to eight students, to facilitate quick grouping for classroom activities or to reinforce bus route numbers during the first week of school. K-1 students should wear name tags at all times during the first week, including wearing them home and bringing them back (a first homework assignment). This will help you learn names quickly. Be prepared to make new name tags for those students who do not get them back to school. Remember that being lost is a terrifying experience for a young student. *Preparing name tags is a must.*

K-2: Bus graph. A good first-day activity is to make a large graph of what buses the students ride. Put this up as a wall display, and use it as a reference when dismissing students. You also might want to have each student make a bus with rotating wheels and copy his or her route number onto it. This could be taken home and used as a reminder each day.

K-6: Name tags for permanent seats. If your students have permanent seats, make name tags or have older students make their own to go on the desks or tables as well. Cover these with clear Con-Tact paper or laminate them. One of the first things you want to accomplish the first day of school is to learn all the students' names. Since most of us are visual learners, the more visual clues you give yourself, the better. Also, your students will have a sense of belonging if they see their names in use. See the section on name games in Chapter 4 for some ideas on ways to have students learn each others' names. Keep these name tags for use throughout the year when substitutes or guest speakers come to your class.

K-2: Name cards. Name cards for classroom use can be made from sentence strip tagboard. Remember to have extra ones cut for those students who arrive on the first day who are not on your roll. You can use these for a variety of activities, from taking roll, to name games, to use for assessment, to choosing who goes where when. For the first few weeks, first names only should be used.

Display the names in a pocket chart or pinned to a bulletin board. As students enter they can find their own names and then move their cards to a designated place to indicate they have arrived. This is a quick and easy way to take roll. If you have another prepared pocket chart with "Hot/Cold Lunch" labels, students can make a daily graph of the lunch count. One of your classroom jobs could be to re-place the name cards in their original spot at the end of the day.

In K-1, students might read the names each day as a whole group. One of the first things students learn to read is each other's names. Making this a routine provides many opportunities for teaching phonics in context.

K-6: Calendar. The classroom calendar should be up and ready to go. This calendar and its related activities constitute a routine you want to establish. It is relatively easy to get together and can be a 10-20-minute activity done every day. See the section on the calendar routine in Chapter 2 for how to set one up.

K-2: Preselected read-alouds. These should be short, with good illustrations, and predictable, repetitive text. Having these preselected and within easy reach of the whole-group area will help with those moments that need to be filled. See the section on read-alouds in Chapter 8 for a bibliography.

3-6: Preselected read-alouds. Books that you really enjoy and that will capture the interest of your students make reading aloud an enjoyable part of the day.

K-2: Written list of fingerplays and songs. You should memorize and be ready with a repertoire of at least 10 songs and fingerplays. See Chapter 5 for some easy ones. Student attention is more easily and gently gained through chanting and singing than through overt phrases such as "I need your attention." If you start a chant, soon all the students will join in.

K-6: Lesson plan book. Set up your plan book with dates for the year (look at a school calendar and put the starting and ending dates of the weeks of school at the top of the pages in your plan book, and list all holidays). At the first teachers' meeting you will probably receive various other important dates to remember. If you have your plan book set up, you can immediately transfer those important dates and responsibilities into your book so you don't forget them. The following are some examples:

- yard duty for each week (This is important. Put this right next to the date at the top of the page in red ink.)
- Back-to-School Night
- parent conferences
- vacation days
- SBC (School Based Curriculum) days
- vision/hearing screenings
- special events
- testing schedule
- report card deadlines
- release time

Having the schedule set up ahead of time will relieve you of trying to find that calendar of events in your piles of papers. This is a good habit to get into: Every time you receive a piece of paper in your box with an important date, you have a place to write it down where you will remember to look at it!

When you set up your plan book, leave a space or column for a "things to do and places to go" list. List your major preparation here. Also list meeting times and places, so you don't forget them.

K-6: File folder for each student. Write each student's name on a file folder and alphabetize the folders by first names. Have the files easily accessible in an open box or tub. Keep extra folders on hand for new arrivals. Having your folders ready will enable you to file quickly those beginning-of-the-year activities that you want to save (e.g., self-portraits, writing samples, teacher observations, parent notes).

K-6: Homework tub or system. Set up a tub where students put their homework, notes from home, permission and other forms, and the like. Keep this in a consistent place near the door.

1-6: Individual work folders. Make each student a construction-paper folder labeled with his or her name. All daily work can be corrected or checked and filed. These folders should be kept in a central location, not in individual student desks. All work can be compiled and sent home on Friday or Monday for review and signature by parents. This provides one night a week of homework and the opportunity for parents to see their children's progress over a week's time.

K-6: Bulletin boards. Create a learning environment that is interesting, inviting, and comfortable. Bulletin boards should reflect the atmosphere you want to have in your classroom.

- Leave at least one blank board for the display of an initial classroom project.
- Plan a welcome-type bulletin board (e.g., "Famous Fourth Graders": put up pictures, names, interview information).
- Use your bulletin boards to tie into the beginning-of-the-year themes.

Many districts have teacher centers where you can use a die-cut machine to cut the letters that you need for bulletin boards. Teacher supply stores also may have prepackaged commercial bulletin boards that would fit in. Remember, however, that to obtain maximum advantage from bulletin boards, you should involve students in the design, layout, and especially the content.

ESSENTIAL KNOWLEDGE

Be sure you know how to find the following:

- classroom key
- classroom light switch
- classroom heat control
- intercom

Academics

- cumulative records
- diagnostic/placement tests
- grade book
- grade-level/subject expectations
- library/texts/workbooks
- plan book
- profiles/individual records
- report cards
- science/math manipulatives
- standardized test results
- student/home information

Equipment/Machinery

- computers/diskettes/printer/paper
- cooking wares/stove
- desks/chairs/tables
- ditto machine/thermal machine
- easels/chalkboards
- electrical outlets
- film projector/screen/extension cords
- films/slides/videos
- filmstrip projector
- filmstrips
- laminator
- overhead projector
- overhead projector pens and plastics
- pencil sharpener
- photocopier/photocopier key
- slide projector
- tape recorder
- video equipment and supplies

Personnel (Name/Schedule/Location)

- aide(s)
- cafeteria staff
- custodians

- fellow teachers
- GATE (Gifted and Talented Education) staff
- migrant personnel
- nurse
- secretary/office personnel
- special education staff
- speech specialists
- yard duty staff

Procedures

- abuse/neglect reporting
- bus rules/procedures
- cafeteria rules
- class rules
- evacuation of building
- field trips
- fire/disaster plan
- fire extinguisher
- library/hall passes
- location of all schedules
- lunch/money/tickets/charges
- petty cash
- phone procedures
- playground rules
- power outage
- roll sheet
- seating chart
- student/aide illness
- substitutes: number/plans
- supply/purchase orders
- weekly bulletin

Supplies

- art supplies
- chalk, chalkboard erasers
- cleaning supplies: broom, dustpan, sponge, soap
- clipboards

- crayons
- ditto/thermal masters
- envelopes
- file folders
- first-aid kit
- hole punch
- Kleenex
- label-making gun and tape
- P.E. equipment: whistle, stopwatch
- paper: butcher, construction, ditto, scratch, writing, tagboard
- paper clips
- paper towels
- paste/glue
- pencils/erasers/pens
- pins
- Post-it Notes
- rubber bands
- rulers
- scissors
- staplers/staples
- stickers
- tape: Scotch, masking
- white board/dry-erase markers, erasers

2 Daily Routines and Procedures

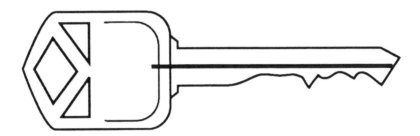

Consistent daily routines will help students feel comfortable and know what to expect. Clear procedures will help students know exactly what behavior is expected in the various learning situations you create.

CHAPTER CONTENTS

CARDINAL RULES OF CLASSROOM MANAGEMENT

Remember the cardinal rules of classroom management: *Model, practice, focus on the positive,* and *be consistent!!*

The following sections outline procedures for various classroom management areas that must be in place in order for you to be successful. These are the "hidden systems" you may not have been aware of in your observations of classrooms or in your student teaching. We urge you to read them carefully, implement them as outlined, and keep at it until your students have learned them.

Creating procedures helps you think through your behavioral expectations for any given activity. That way, you are able to communicate those expectations clearly to the students and thus prevent disruptions. You can either tell the students your expectations for a specific procedure or have the class develop them under your guidance.

FREEZE AND LISTEN

This is a must. You need to decide what signal you will use to notify your students that they must stop, look, and listen to an adult. This could be a bell, a chord on the piano, a note sounded on a xylophone, a hand signal—whatever you choose. In kindergarten and first grade, it is useful to have the students do an accompanying body motion when they hear the signal (e.g., hands in the air, hands on head). It is also effective to start a chant or song to accompany cleanup. For example, you can sing, to the tune of "The Farmer in the Dell," "It's time to clean up, it's time to clean up. Heigh ho the derry-o, it's time to clean up. Es hora de limpiar, es hora de limpiar. Que viva la escuela, es hora de limpiar." Putting a soothing record on also facilitates calm when returning to the whole group.

Starting from the first day, at the first transition, you must model, role-play, and practice this procedure over and over. It is critical that all the adults in the room model the desired behavior along with the students. At the first class meeting, explain the procedure—a visual is helpful (e.g., a picture of a bell, above a stop sign, above big eyes, above big ears) to use as you explain (see Figure 2.1). At the first whole-group meeting, you might do the following to model the procedure (note that the language in this example is designed for a K-2 class; you will need to adapt it for grades 3-6).

Say, "Today we're going to practice what we do when we hear this sound. First, Alicia [the teacher's aide] and I will show you what to do." You then choose a child to be the "teacher" and whisper in his or her ear what he or she is to do—for example, let you talk and color for a few moments, and then ring a bell. You pretend to be coloring and talking with Alicia until your "teacher" rings the bell or gives whatever other freeze-and-listen signal you have chosen. At that point you must model exactly what you want the kids to do: *Freeze* and *look at the "teacher."*

Next, call up a small group of students to role-play what you and your aide just did. Your aide can take the role-play group away to review what they are going to

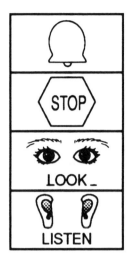

Figure 2.1. Sample Freeze-and-Listen Visual

do, while you give the others the task of being the observers and watching for the proper behavior. Have the role-players pretend to be busy. Make your freeze-and-listen signal, and *praise, praise, praise* when they comply. Encourage the audience to praise also.

Now you're ready to have the whole class role-play. Have them stay in the circle and pretend to be busy coloring, talking quietly to their neighbors. Make your freeze-and-listen signal. Your aide should be instructed to go to noncompliers and quietly remind them of the procedure. You should focus on giving positive praise to those who are complying and to the whole class when all comply.

Review the procedure with the students using the visual. This activity should take 10-15 minutes and should be followed by something active.

This procedure will have to be practiced often—at every transition for the first week or so. That means you should continue to have your aide or parent volunteer involved, continue to praise, and continue to redirect those students having a hard time learning the procedure. Spending time and energy putting this procedure firmly in place will pay huge dividends later.

CLEANUP

In an active, interactive classroom, your students must be responsible for the maintenance of the environment. Several different types of cleanup need to be considered.

Individual responsibilities. The rule is to clean up after yourself. During the first few days of school, include this in any modeling you do. For example, if you are doing a cut-and-paste art project and are explaining the how to, be sure to include the how to of cleanup in your explanation—where to put your scissors when you've finished, where scraps go, and so on. As you review the project after completion, make special note to compliment the students' efforts at cleanup.

The success of cleanup will depend on your having clearly marked areas for supplies that are easily accessible to the students. Remember the decisions you made about materials. Make sure the students know their responsibilities. Students must know what to do after they have cleaned up their own work space (e.g., sit at the whole-group area and wait quietly, or go to their seat and look at a book).

Classroom responsibilities. These cleanup duties involve such tasks as keeping the book corner neat, washing the tables, and taking the roll to the office. It is

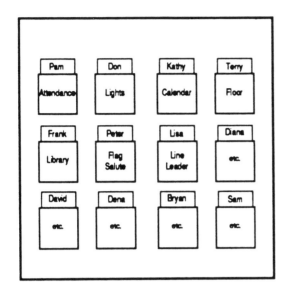

Figure 2.2. Jobs Chart

helpful to have a "jobs chart" that lists the tasks that need to be done on a daily basis, but in which not everyone needs to participate. Such a chart could take many different forms (an example of one format is shown in Figure 2.2); however, the most important aspects are that students are trained in what the jobs entail, that jobs are rotated in a fair manner, and that you are consistent in making students accountable for completing their jobs. Some possible classroom jobs for students are library monitor, light monitor, office monitor, leader of cleanup, leader of games, leader for the flag salute, pencils monitor, and line leader.

The students can participate in the development of the jobs chart by brainstorming what jobs need to be done. Don't do this the first day of school, but shortly thereafter. Again, role-play, model, and reinforce what is expected for each job. This could be done as an inclusion activity in which you divide the class and have each group learn one job and teach it to a partner.

Special project cleanup responsibilities. When you plan a messy activity, consider how you can involve the students in cleanup. Often, the cleanup of these projects falls to you or your aide. Include cleanup procedures in the explanation of the project and review them with students before beginning to work on the project.

PROCEDURES FOR LESSONS, GROUPS, AND ROTATIONS

Teacher-Directed Whole-Class Lesson

Procedures for a teacher-directed lesson with the whole class may vary depending on the kind of lesson involved. You may want to require that desks are cleared off or that certain materials are out on the desks. Use your freeze-and-listen signal to get attention.

You want to have clear procedures for the kind of attention you expect (chairs turned to face you, eyes looking at you, students may be drawing while you are talking, or whatever). Think them through and make them clear and reasonable (for example, consider what to tell students to do if they can't see or hear, or if they need to sharpen a pencil). Spell the procedures out clearly.

SAMPLE PROCEDURE CHART FOR A
TEACHER-DIRECTED WHOLE-CLASS LESSON

---

(1) Clear desk and stay in your seat.
(2) One person talks at a time.
(3) Raise your hand to speak.
(4) Focus on (look at!) the speaker.
(5) Follow teacher directions.

---

(1) Quita todo de encima de tu escritorio y quédate en tu asiento.
(2) Sólo una persona habla a la vez.
(3) Levanta la mano para hablar.
(4) Fíjate en el orador. (Mírale al orador.)
(5) Sigue las instrucciones de la maestra.

Teacher-Directed Whole Group on the Floor/Rug

In kindergarten, most whole-group instruction is done with the students sitting on the floor. In first and second grade this is still true, but some instruction is done with students sitting at their seats. For this type of instruction, see the procedures outlined above.

For whole-group floor procedures, the following should be practiced from the first day of school:

- Students should know where and how to sit. Some teachers prefer a circle arrangement. If you elect this arrangement, mark the circle on the floor with tape to delineate its size and where students should sit.

- Some teachers prefer a group with an undefined shape or rows. If you use rows, again mark the rug or floor with tape. For an undefined arrangement, you need to delineate the boundaries of the group space in some way—often furniture will do this, but you must make it clear to your students what is out-of-bounds (e.g., being under a piece of furniture or behind a chair).

- It is important to practice the "how to" of sitting on the floor. Don't use the term *Indian style*—avoid stereotyping. Instead, show the students the cross-legged position expected at floor time. Use a chant such as "I sit on the floor by myself, crisscross" to remind them of the expectation, instead of singling out individuals. Again, use your aide to help individually those having a hard time.

- Decide and tell your students how you expect them to respond to questions or to join in discussions—raise hands, shout out, wait until someone has finished speaking, or whatever. This may vary from activity to activity, but should be made clear at the beginning of each activity.

Small-Group Teacher-Directed Lesson

The teacher will be working with a small group while the rest of the class is working either independently or in other small groups with learning assistants (adults or cross-age helpers), cooperatively, or whatever. Before going to work with a small group, set the rules for the other groups in the class—what if they need to use the bathroom, don't have a pencil, or have a question? All problems should have procedures, so that, short of a minor disaster, you are free to work with your small group.

In your small group, set procedures for how students are to come to the work area, what they should bring, what transition activity they are to do while waiting for the directed group to start, how they are to respond in a discussion (informally, raising hands, and so on), and, if supplies are at the workstation, who distributes them, who collects them, and what procedures are to be followed in leaving the workstation.

SAMPLE PROCEDURE CHART FOR A SMALL-GROUP TEACHER-DIRECTED LESSON

(1) Come quietly to group with materials.
(2) Follow directions on board for transition activity.
(3) Give attention to speaker in the group.
(4) Raise hand to speak unless it's open discussion.
(5) Put station materials away and clean up before leaving.
(6) Return quietly to your own seat and begin work.

---

(1) Ven calladito a tu grupo con tus materiales.
(2) Sigue las direcciones en el pizarrón para la actividad transitoria.
(3) Fija tu atención en el orador del grupo.
(4) Levanta la mano para hablar a menos de que sea una discusión abierta.
(5) Antes de irte, guarda los materiales y limpia la estación.
(6) Regresa calladito a tu propio escritorio y comienza a trabajar.

Small-Group Rotations

Usually a teacher sets up some kind of rotation system to ensure that he or she sees each student on a regular basis and has the opportunity to provide direct instruction to small groups. It is critical to train your students in the rotation system you choose before doing any in-depth content.

You need to think through the organization of any rotation times you will schedule. For example, during an hour-long language arts period you might want to see two groups for one-half hour each. That would mean that in a class with four groups you would see each student every other day. Or you may wish to see each group every day. Therefore, you would need a two-hour block for language arts or would see each group for only 15 minutes. Once you have decided for how long you will see each group, you have other decisions to make:

- What kind of adult help do you have? What will their responsibilities be? What kind of system will you use to tell them what to do?
- How will the students be grouped? By language, by ability, heterogeneously by language?
- What will the non-teacher-directed activities be? Journals, spelling, workbooks, handwriting, listening center, oral reading?
- Will you use cross-age tutors? Which activities are appropriate for them to work with?
- Will students always rotate with the same groups, or will they be divided differently for independent workstations?
- Where will you meet with students? Where will the aides, tutors, and parent volunteers meet with students?

Once you have made these decisions, you can begin to formulate a plan. Sit down with a piece of paper, a class list, and your assessment information if you wish. On a blank piece of paper, make a grid with the number of rotations you will have down one side and the activities you have across the top. For example:

| | Teacher   Aide | Independent | Listening |
	Directed Lesson	Cut and Paste Game	Book and Tape
8:30- 9:00			
9:00- 9:30			
9:30-10:00			
10:00-10:30			

This would be a four-group rotation, with the teacher seeing each student every day. Once you have your time schedule and activities down, you can begin to group your students. We recommend heterogeneous grouping as opposed to skill-level grouping.

In a bilingual situation the only limitation during a language arts time will be language of instruction. You will need to have your students in groups based on whether they are learning literacy concepts in English or Spanish. In math, social studies, and other subjects, however, languages may be mixed.

Divide your class as nearly as you can into four equally numbered groups. Name each group (number, color, animal; see Figure 2.3). This is just for the purposes of figuring out the rotation. Once groups have been established, a good team-building activity is for them to name themselves. You can then begin to fill in the rotation scheme.

What colors would go in the listening column in Figure 2.3? If you thought Green, Blue, Red, and then Yellow, you're on your way to developing systems. This is the simplest system; students stay with the same group throughout the rotation schedule. This is a good place to start.

Now that you know what will happen, you need to teach the rotation and what is expected at each "station." Plan on spending at least two weeks being the facilitator in this learning by easing into a full rotation system. In other words, don't plan to spend time with your small group—you will be roaming, praising, answering questions, keeping students on task, and so on. You will only be frustrated if you try to do a lesson as well. Have independent work for your group to do. The following outlines a sample strategy for introducing centers:

- Prepare a chart with the students' names listed under the colors of their groups or written on construction paper of the colors of their groups. Post the chart near your whole-group meeting area. (For kindergartners you could also add a photocopied picture of each child next to his or her name.)

- Show the chart to the students at whole-group time. Explain to them how to find which group they belong to. Have several students come up and point to their names. Have the whole group shout out these students' group colors.

- Say, "All students in the Blue Group stand up quietly." Read off the names from your chart and have the students sit down as you call their names. Continue for each group. (In kindergarten, hand out colored yarn necklaces for the students to wear as they determine their group colors. You can use these for a few days to help you and the students learn the groups.)

Now, hopefully, everyone knows his or her group. The next step is to work on the rotation scheme. Shorten the time allotted at each station during the first two weeks of practice. A sample strategy follows:

	Teacher	Aide	Independent	Listening
8:30-9	Blue	Red	Yellow	?
9-9:30	Red	Yellow	Green	?
9:30-10	Yellow	Green	Blue	?
10-10:30	Green	Blue	Red	?

Figure 2.3. Sample Rotation Grid

- On the first day of practice, have all your students learn what happens at the teacher center. Say, "When it's your turn to work with me, you will come to the horseshoe table in the back of the classroom. While you wait for me to get everyone settled, you will look at one of the books in the blue box." Have one group role-play this for the whole class.
- Next, move everyone to the next station. Say, "This is where you will work with Alicia [aide]." Explain all items the students should bring with them when coming to this work area, if any. Move through all the stations in this manner. Do it quickly—only an overview at this time.
- Now, introduce a rotation chart, such as the one shown in Figure 2.4, or an individual "map" to be pasted in each student's work folder, such as those shown in Figure 2.5. In whole group, have the students determine where they go for Rotation 1. At your signal, the Blue Group will go to its assigned area, followed by the Red, Green, and Yellow groups, one at a time. When all groups are at their assigned first rotations, make your freeze-and-listen signal. Wait for complete attention, and then have students determine where they go on the second rotation. Model how to rotate: Walk quietly and quickly to where you go. Do this all together by saying, "Everyone stand up. Point to where you go. Now walk quietly to Rotation 2." Repeat for Rotations 3 and 4. Give plenty of praise and encouragement.

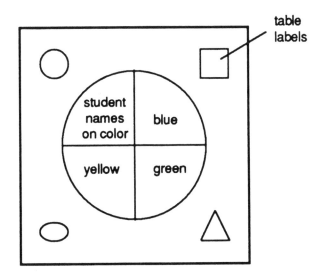

Figure 2.4. Rotation Chart

- Now that students are at Rotation 4, have them go back to Rotation 1 and have an activity planned for them to do.
- The next day, review the rotation scheme in whole group. Use four students from each of the four groups to model. Start with Rotation 1. Have the four role-play students go to their assigned table, and have the other students help you review the signal that will tell them to move. Make the signal and say, "Rotation 2." The role-play students should move accordingly. Other students can applaud. Continue role-playing with Rotations 2, 3, and 4.
- Now you're ready to do a full-scale run. Have group activities prepared and at the centers. Activities should be simple. Remember that your small-group activity should be independent. The more responsibility you can give to your students for figuring out what to do, the better. For example, a directions poster for each center will give them visual clues as to what to do. Directions should rely on pictures and words to get the message across.
- Encourage your students to ask each other for help. *Do not allow yourself to become the sole keeper of knowledge. Be consistent in not answering the questions that students can ask each other.* Explain to your students that when they have questions, they should first ask themselves, then a friend, before they raise their hands to let you know they have questions. Stress the importance of not interrupting the teacher when he or she is teaching. This is part of developing a love for learning—the most important element in the classroom is having respect for that process.

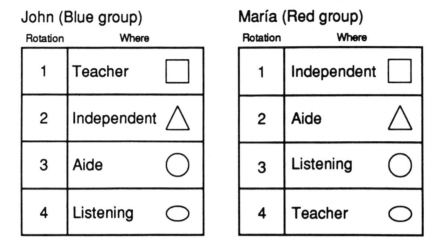

Figure 2.5. Individual Student Rotation "Maps"

- Dismiss each group in turn to go to Rotation 1. You should roam and give specific praise, help any students who have a hard time getting started, reinforce work behavior, and so on.

- When it is time to move to Rotation 2, make your freeze-and-listen signal. Review cleanup, where they move, and so on. Say, "You have two minutes to clean up and be ready to move. I will know you're ready to move when I see your whole group sitting quietly with folders in front of you and your eyes on me." Wait until you see that. Then have everyone get up and move to the next station.

- Repeat for Rotations 3 and 4. You will probably need to do this for the entire first week. The goal is to establish this routine clearly so you do not need to be involved and can devote your attention to your small group without interruption. You can expect to be able to do this only if you practice, practice, practice the first few weeks of school.

Independent Workers

Spend several weeks training students on independent work. Think through exactly which behaviors will be acceptable during independent work time, and write up a chart explaining these—for instance, will you allow students to talk, to get out of their seats, to ask others for help? What if they need help to sharpen a pencil, get a drink of water, or go to the bathroom? What do they do when they finish their work? Set the procedures, and leave yourself free to monitor behavior. This means that if you're practicing independent time and they need help, you do not help them; instead, you have them follow the procedures that are set up. The following chart has example procedures.

SAMPLE PROCEDURE CHART FOR INDEPENDENT WORKERS

(1) Work by yourself or with a partner.

(2) Focus on the assigned work.

(3) Whisper if you need to ask a question.

(4) Follow cooperative group procedures if you have a question: (a) Ask yourself, (b) ask a neighbor, (c) ask someone at another table.

(5) Do not interrupt the teacher.

---

(1) Trabaja sólo o con un/a compañero/a.

(2) Fíjate en el trabajo asignado.

(3) Usa voz baja si necesitas hacer una pregunta.

(4) Sigue el proceso de grupos cooperativos si tienes alguna pregunta: (a) Pregúntate, (b) pregúntale a un vecino, (c) pregúntale a alguien en otra mesa.

(5) No le interrumpas a la maestra.

Cooperative Learning Groups

Teach a *zero-noise hand signal* before beginning any cooperative groups. When you raise your hand, students are to (a) raise their hands, (b) get quiet, and (c) tap the shoulders of others around them to get quiet. Practice this many times throughout the day over several days before beginning cooperative learning groups.

Positive praise. Teach words for use in praising one another. Brainstorm words on the board so that students have words of their own to use. Add to the list throughout the year. Keep the list handy for students to refer to. Role-play, practice, and reward usage of praise words.

Individual/group rewards. Students will continue to need to be rewarded for individual efforts as well as for group efforts. They should receive rewards for processes, procedures, and activities, as well as for products. Rewards can be anything from verbal praise, smiles, and pats on the back to points, raffles, and other tangible rewards. See the section on reward systems.

Cooperative work should include (a) "class-building" activities to build class unity, (b) group- or team-building activities, and (c) partner activities. Having students work in pairs is an effective way to introduce content-packed activities such as reading, writing, research, or math work in a cooperative approach.

During the first month of school, teacher attention during cooperative activities should be focused on the procedures and interactions, *not on content.* Processing should occur during each cooperative activity to reflect on what was successful and to generalize the learning to other experiences. Processing questions for a group discussion might include the following:

- Why was your group successful/unsuccessful in completing the task?
- Did you listen to your group?
- Did you develop any strategy for coming to a decision when people disagreed?
- How could you use that strategy on the playground or at home?

Class Meetings

Class meetings can be used for problem solving, topic discussions, determining class rules, deciding class functions, team-building activities, and positive interactions.

During these meetings, everyone sits in a circle, either on the floor or on chairs, so that all participants can have eye contact. Have the class practice getting into and out of the class-meeting circle (arrange desks, chairs, and so on) following the established procedures. Give students specific praise about what they did well each time. With practice, this should take one to two minutes.

The students may add items to the agenda as they deem necessary. The location for the agenda should be constant (a section of the chalkboard, a hanging clipboard). Keep minutes of the meeting to refer to. Teach students to make "I" statements, such as "I don't like so much noise during writer's workshop" instead of "John and Benito are talking too much." End with a compliment circle to close the meeting on a positive note. Model effective social skills.

SAMPLE PROCEDURE CHART FOR CLASS MEETINGS

---

(1) Sit with bottoms on the floor (or all four legs of chair on floor).
(2) Come empty-handed.
(3) One person talks at a time; raise your hand to speak.
(4) Focus on the speaker.
(5) Participate.
(6) You have the right to pass on a discussion.
(7) Stay in the circle until the meeting is over.

---

(1) Siéntate en el suelo (o con las cuatro patas de la silla en el suelo).
(2) Deja todo en tu escritorio.
(3) Levanta la mano para hablar; sólo una persona habla a la vez.
(4) Fíjate en el orador.
(5) Participa.
(6) Tienes el derecho de no contribuir a la discusión.
(7) Quédate en tu lugar en el círculo hasta que la junta termine.

STRATEGIES REGARDING BEHAVIOR

Promoting Good Behavior

If you've put all the previous information in place and still feel your management is not what it should be, we have some additional strategies you might employ:

- *Use "surprise" reinforcers.* Periodically, without warning, schedule a surprise for your class. Tell them the surprise is a direct result of their good behavior. For example, you might cancel a test, extend P.E., have a special art project, or show a video.

- *Vary your lessons.* Often disruptions occur because a task took too long. Determine the length of your students' attention span and plan a change of task. Alternate activities that require large motor movements with those that are quieter.

- *Build relationships with your students.* Students are more willing to cooperate with people they like. Get to know them as individuals—use plenty of praise. Tell them what they do well. This is particularly effective with students with whom you are having difficulty. Force yourself to find out about those students so you can relate to them on a personal and positive level. Talk about topics they're interested in.

- *Be a good example.* Model the type of behavior you expect from your students. Model active listening, being prepared, thoughtfulness, and the like. Share your experiences with your students. Tell them how you've handled personal frustrations or how you enjoyed a book you just read.

- *Create an exciting curriculum.* Get the students involved in activities and discussions instead of passively listening and responding. This requires a lot of preparation and planning, but it can reduce disruptions.

Correcting Misbehavior

Occasionally you will need to correct a misbehaving student. Here are some strategies to consider.

- *Look for simple solutions.* Make a list of specific inappropriate behaviors, then look for solutions. For example, if two students continue to talk, separate their desks. If students come late to class, use a stopwatch and deduct the time from their next break. Sometimes students are able to brainstorm solutions to particular problems during class meetings.

- *Reinforce your procedures consistently.* Be specific about your behavioral expectations and post them. Use a reward system (see the next section). Have the consequences of disruptive behavior already thought out. Decide how you will record good and bad behavior (e.g., individually, by tables, or whole class, using tallies, stars, or stickers). Explain your plan to your students and follow through the first time a student misbehaves.

- *Reward good behavior.* Verbally praise the specific behavior you want to reinforce. For instance, "Ruth is following directions" or "Fred cleaned up his desk and is ready to listen" is more specific than "I like the way Ruth is helping" or "Good job, Fred." Catch the students being good, especially those who misbehave most.

- *Write behavior contracts.* If a certain student constantly disrupts the class, write a contract with him or her that is specific and appropriate to the misbehavior. The contract should include (a) the desired behavior (e.g., raising hand before talking), (b) how often the behavior must occur (e.g., 100% of the time), (c) the reinforcer (e.g., a 10-minute break in class each day), and (d) the term of the contract (e.g., a week or less). Note that this contract should be developed *with* the student, especially the reinforcer.

- *Report to parents.* These reports are most effective if they are positive. Call the parents and tell them how well their child is doing/behaving in class. If after you've tried a contract with no change in student behavior, enlist parent support. Often parents can help determine reinforcers (e.g., extra TV time, special family event) or consequences (e.g., no skateboarding, no TV).

Remember: A positive classroom environment requires consistency, modeling, and practice. It does not happen magically.

Reward Systems

There are a variety of ways you may choose to reward your students to reinforce their following of procedures. Reward systems are used initially to motivate students to try to succeed at a new behavior. The system is kept in place until mastery of the desired behavior has occurred, and then it is phased out. Edible rewards (popcorn, raisins), tangible rewards (stickers, prizes), and tokens (points, tickets) are all low-level reinforcers. Our goal in using reward systems is to develop internal motivation in our students. Vary the rewards over time. Following are some ideas:

- *The marble jar.* The class earns marbles for good behavior, and these are displayed in a jar. When the jar is filled, the class has earned a special privilege, such as a party or the chance to watch a video. Start with a small jar.

- *Secret words.* The teacher determines a positive consequence for the class and a secret word to be spelled. When the class earns a letter for good behavior, it is put on the bulletin board. When the word is spelled, the class receives the consequence (e.g., popcorn, free play, video, picnic, party).

- *Grab bags.* Individuals earn points through academic work or behavior. A certain number of points lets them pick an object or certificate (e.g., the chance to be a team leader or special monitor, extra free time, a free homework pass).

- *Rent classroom valuables.* Through appropriate behavior students can rent classroom objects such as puzzles, games, special books, or toys for overnight or weekend use.

- *Raffle/auction.* Students earn raffle tickets for appropriate behavior. After a period of time, students bring objects from home, with their parents' permission, and hold a raffle.

- *Preferred activity time (PAT).* Give the whole class unconditional time for academically related games (15-20 minutes for Around the World, Jeopardy, Spelling or Math Baseball, or the like). The time can be taken away from the whole class for misbehavior, or from individuals who don't finish work or constantly disrupt.

DAILY ONGOING ACTIVITIES

Silent Reading

Set clear procedures for silent reading (for K-1, this should be called *quiet reading*, and students should be allowed to share and converse quietly about their books). Have students choose the books they will read before going to recess or lunch, and have them waiting on their desks when they come in, or have boxes of books at each table. If a student chooses short, simple books, have two or three on the desk so he or she won't have to get up. In lower grades start silent reading in short intervals, increasing the time each day to 20-30 minutes.

During the first few weeks, use this opportunity to assess students. Walk around and note names of books and page numbers each day to see if students are moving through their books. Ask students to read quietly to you from their books and ask some simple questions to determine their levels of understanding. Don't verbalize any judgments to them about books being too hard or too easy. During silent reading they may read whatever they want. Use the information you gather to suggest books that they may enjoy at the library or at other times in class. Work toward being able to sit down and read a book yourself during silent reading time. This makes a strong statement to students.

SAMPLE PROCEDURE CHART FOR SILENT READING

(1) Have a book (two or three if they're short) on your desk before going out to recess.

(2) Come in without talking and get your book.

(3) Remain in your seat, or find a spot on the floor.

(4) Read to yourself without disturbing anyone.

(5) If you finish early, begin your next book.

(6) When silent reading is over, you may share something you enjoyed.

---

(1) Antes de salir al recreo, deja un libro en tu escritorio (dos o tres si son cortos).

(2) Entra sin hablar y agarra tu libro.

(3) Quédate en tu asiento o encuentra un espacio en el suelo.

(4) Lee en silencio sin molestar a nadie.

(5) Si terminas un libro, comienza a leer el otro.

(6) Cuando se termine el tiempo de leer en silencio, puedes compartir algo que te gustó de lo que leíste.

Read-Alouds

Daily exposure to quality literature increases the desire to read independently and models many reading skills. Schedule 10-15 minutes for primary and 20-30 minutes for older students. In bilingual classes, don't be afraid to read stories in students' second language; think in terms of emerging comprehension. Give visual cues and use strategies such as alternate day and preview/review. See the section on strategies for bilingual classes below.

Sometimes discuss the story with the class; predict, clarify vocabulary in context, analyze the plot, and visualize the setting. Don't overdo the discussion—remember that your main purpose is for them to enjoy the author's work. Don't analyze every story.

Preview the book before beginning with the class. Look for appropriateness to grade level (length of passages, vocabulary, interest), and familiarize yourself with characters and points to be highlighted.

When creating procedures for read-aloud time, think about the following questions:

- Where will the students sit?
- May they draw or write, or do you want them looking at you?
- May they get up and sharpen pencils, get a drink of water, or the like?

The following chart of sample procedures assumes that you will allow the children to draw while they listen to you read.

SAMPLE PROCEDURE CHART FOR READ-ALOUD

(1) Get all materials for drawing before reading begins.
(2) Stay seated while the teacher is reading.
(3) Listen silently to the story.
(4) Clean up at the end of the read-aloud time.

(1) Agara todo el material de dibujar antes de que comienza la maestra a leer.
(2) Manténte sentado mientras la maestra esté leyéndole al grupo.
(3) Escucha en silencio al cuento.
(4) Recoge todo cuando la lectura en voz alta termine.

Journals

Journals may be created by stapling several sheets of paper into a construction-paper folder. For beginning writers, a large drawing space with a few lines underneath is great. By third or fourth grade, the drawing space can be eliminated. Journals are places for students to write their thoughts on a daily basis, with content being important, not mechanics. Creative spelling should be encouraged by not spelling for students. Journals may be interactive; that is, the teacher may write back to the students.

Journal writing, like any activity, must be modeled. A teacher can do this by writing right alongside students. Reading from a personal journal as well as reading from journals of historians, writers, and others are good models for students. You can also demonstrate the process on an overhead projector to show that journal writing is just writing down thoughts.

SAMPLE PROCEDURE CHART FOR JOURNALS

(1) Write for 10 minutes silently.

(2) Write about anything you like or choose a topic from the board.

(3) Don't worry about punctuation.

(4) Invent your own spelling.

(5) Stay in your seat.

---

(1) Escribe en silencio por diez minutos.

(2) Escribe de cualquiera cosa o escoge un tema del pizarrón.

(3) No te preocupes por la puntuación.

(4) Inventa como deletrear las palabras.

(5) Quédate en tu asiento.

Literature Logs

Literature logs are similar to journals, but rather than writing on any topic, students respond to literature. They may respond to the read-aloud or to their own silent reading. Their logs may reflect class discussions or just their own private reactions.

Calendar, K-2

The purpose of doing a calendar routine is to provide real-life math experiences for your students. It usually requires 10 to 20 minutes per day. As students learn the procedures, provide for some rotation so each student can be the leader. Choosing a "captain" or "helper" to help you each day allows you to become the facilitator.

Figure 2.6 illustrates various ideas for the calendar. Choose the ones you feel are appropriate to your grade level and in which you can maintain interest. Keep your calendar time simple, flexible, and interesting. As you add new items to the calendar, be sure you model them.

Setting up the calendar takes some time at the beginning of the year, but most parts will stay up all year, with just a few monthly changes. The following lists the specific things you will need for each part of the calendar bulletin board. The letters correspond to the illustrations in Figure 2.6.

A: *Month pattern grid calendar.* The month calendar grid is displayed with only the name of the month and the days of the week at the beginning of a month. The grid should contain squares of about 3 × 3 inches. Each day, add

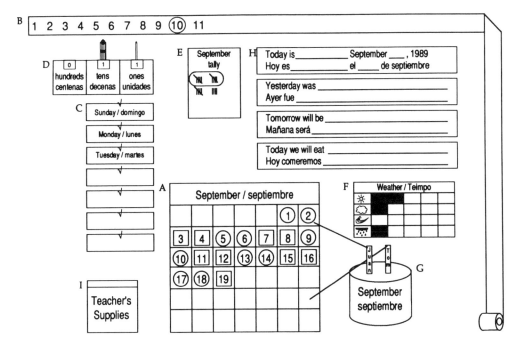

Figure 2.6. Calendar Ideas

the marker that corresponds to the date. You need to make daily markers to fit the grid squares based on a pattern (e.g., shapes, seasonal cutouts, color). Keep the daily markers in the teacher supply container (see the explanation of I, below). Use this to reinforce the date, the pattern, and the days of the week.

B: *Days of school graph.* Use adding-machine tape with a string tied through the roll so it can be pinned to the wall. Record with black each day you are in school, marking the 10s in a red pen and circling them. This graph can be used for daily rote counting activities as well as development of the understanding of the pattern of the base 10 number system.

C: *Days of the week.* Make 3 × 8-inch strips of tagboard with the days of the week written on them. Punch a hole in the center of each card so it can be hung from a pin and easily turned over. Turn over only those days that have already passed. This activity is done in conjunction with a days of the week song (see Chapter 5). Talk about how many days have gone by in a week and how many are yet to come. Responses can be written in number sentence form (e.g., 3 + 4 = 7).

D: *Number line straw box.* Use three half-gallon milk cartons cut down to 4 inches high. Cover these with Con-Tact paper (in three different colors if you want to make the place value more visual). Label the boxes "ones," "tens," and "hundreds." Attach a set of flip numerals to each carton. The straw count will match the days of school graph. Add one straw each day, bundling the tens as they occur. Use this to count by tens and ones with your students.

E: *Monthly tally.* Use a 9 × 12-inch piece of newsprint or a small chalkboard nailed to your bulletin board. Make a tally mark for each day of the month, circling the tens. The tally count corresponds to the monthly calendar. Count the tally marks each day, using the tens or fives as a starting point. Ask prediction questions, such as "How many more days until we can circle a 10 again? A group of 5?"

F: *Weather graph.* Make a grid with pictures for sunny, cloudy, rainy, and so on on the left side and at least 15 squares across. Each day, have the captain or leader determine the weather outside and color a square next to the appropriate type of weather. At the end of the month a total tally can be made. Display the graphs of each month and use them for an analysis of how the weather changes over the year.

G: *Birthday graph.* Before the beginning of school, prepare a birthday cake or similar representation for each month of the school year. If you use a birthday cake, have each student write (or you write) his or her birthday on a candle. After discussing the birthday graph, use the 12 cakes and candles for a permanent bulletin board display. Put the "cake of the month" on the calendar bulletin board, with the appropriate students' candles, and use yarn (roving) to indicate where each birthday falls on the monthly calendar.

H: *Date/menu strips.* Use sentence strip tagboard to make the sentences shown in Figure 2.6. Make day of the week cards to fit the blanks, as well as month and numeral cards to fit the blank spaces. Also, make cards for the main-dish items on your school menu. The captain can find these cards, read the menu and select the appropriate card, then read the completed sentences or choose someone to read the sentences when the cards have been placed.

I: *Teacher supplies.* Use a Ziploc bag or small box stapled to the bulletin board to store the supplies you will need to do the calendar: black and red wide felt-tip pens, the date markers for the monthly calendar, the day of the week cards for the date strips, extra pins, and so on.

STRATEGIES FOR BILINGUAL CLASSES

It is very important in a bilingual class to create equal status for both languages and to promote bilingualism. It is significant to the self-concept of the LEP student to see Spanish being valued and to feel comfortable and successful in developing skill in his or her first language. It is also crucial for English speakers to value and learn Spanish for the greater goal of a pluralistic society and to maintain integrated bilingual classrooms. (What's in it for English-speaking students if they're not learning Spanish?) Without equal status of languages, negative stereotyping results.

From the very first day, the unique character of a bilingual class should be promoted. Bilingual students should be valued as translators. English-only and Spanish-only students should be valued as models of their native languages. The following are some strategies to help create a truly bilingual atmosphere.

Alternate Day/Week

On alternating days/weeks, Spanish is used in the opening of the day, calendar, general instructions, transition instructions, music, art, and P.E. (and possibly math and science). Literacy continues to be taught daily in students' dominant languages. The following days/weeks, English is used in the same way. By using gestures and visual clues as well as relying on their understanding of daily routines, students become second-language learners throughout the day.

Preview/Review

When introducing a story or a content lesson, preview the lesson by telling the class what it will be about and emphasize important points. The preview is done in the language that is not the language of the day/week (let's say English). Then the lesson is done in the language of the day (Spanish). That might mean reading for 15 minutes in Spanish to your whole class. Then review or discuss to make sure students understood in the same language as the preview (English). When you have only one or two students who would not understand the lesson, you might take them aside for the preview. Create ways to include them; for instance, give them props to hold or a role in the story. After the lesson, meet with them again to discuss the lesson.

Cooperative Grouping

Create heterogeneous language groupings. Include a bilingual student in each group to act as translator.

Language Partners

Pair up English and Spanish speakers to practice the same poem or a given set of vocabulary in both languages or to give the same presentation bilingually. You will need to do some cooperation and team-building activities to prepare for this.

Second Language

We have mentioned several approaches to creating situations for second-language learning to occur naturally in the classroom. In addition, most programs require between 20 minutes (K-1) to 50 minutes (6-8) per day of second-language instruction. This may mean a more structured approach to the teaching of a second language. Second-language instruction should occur only in the second language. You will need to teach beginning students some signals they will need to follow directions (e.g., hand to the ear means to listen, hand to the mouth means to respond). Beginning second language should be taught through songs, poems, games, and simple commands to follow and act out.

Second-language learning is usually divided into four levels:

(1) *The receptive level:* Students are learning to understand spoken commands by hearing them and seeing them acted out. Receptive-level students should not be put on the spot to speak, but should be encouraged to use their second language in a nonthreatening way as it develops.

(2) *Beginning speech emergence:* Students are beginning to speak. They will use more nouns and will use verbs in the present tense. Often they have difficulty with sounds of the language. They should be encouraged and praised for trying, not corrected for errors. Learning occurs through modeling, listening opportunities, and practice, not through error correction.

(3) *Intermediate speech emergence:* Students are able to communicate, but still have some difficulty with verb tenses and have limited vocabularies.

(4) *Fluency:* Students can communicate fluently. They generally need more vocabulary development and work on idiomatic expressions.

It is useful to note into which of the above categories a student falls, so that you can focus on his or her stage of development and also assess progress. It does not mean the student must be grouped only with students at that level to progress. There may be times for specific lessons that you divide by skill ability; however, more heterogeneous grouping will allow students to learn and to build confidence from one another.

Second-language learning is an essential component of the bilingual classroom and should begin as quickly as possible. The most effective way to plan what to teach is to tie it in with your thematic units in social studies, science, math, and literature. Decide what common core vocabulary you will promote in both languages and add to the list as the language develops naturally. This will give you valuable documentation and allow you to share students' progress with parents and administrators.

3 The First Day of School . . . A Detailed Account

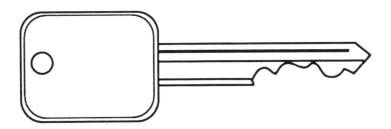

The descriptions of the first day presented in this chapter are meant to give you formats that can be followed on successive days. Remember, these activities are designed to help you (a) get to know your students, (b) create positive attitudes in the class, and (c) train students in routines and procedures.

CHAPTER CONTENTS

THE FIRST DAY OF SCHOOL, K-1

The first day of school in kindergarten or first grade is a challenge. Kindergarten students may be very unsure of themselves. Parents often accompany their children on the first day. Dealing with children's insecurity and their parents' concerns is a major part of the first day. The more adult helpers you can have available, the better. Forewarn the students' parents that you would like them to leave at a certain time, so you can bond with their children. You need to do this gently, but firmly. Students are often very different when their parents are around.

Careful planning will help you get through. Have tables set up with easy puzzles, easy games, paper and crayons, books to look at, and the like. (Don't put out activities that will require a lot of cleanup. Remember, the students haven't been taught how to do it yet.) The students can enter, be greeted by you, and directed to a table to begin exploring. This will give you a chance to reassure parents briefly and to console criers. Have your aide, coteacher, or a trusted parent help you with the inconsolable crier(s)—take them for a walk, to sit on a lap, or whatever helps. Your primary responsibility is to the majority of the students.

In K, plan on having your coteacher work all day with you the first week. Reciprocate during his or her session. If an aide is not scheduled to be with you during your entire session, try to have help for at least the beginning of the day and at the end. Ask around to see if someone (support personnel such as resource teachers or reading specialists, perhaps) could be available at these critical times.

First graders will have overcome some of their first-day fears, but they still are not seasoned schoolers. You still may want to have some activities set up on tables for students to self-select as they arrive so that you can deal with any parents or unforeseen traumas.

The major difficulty with first grade is the longer day. First graders will be very tired after lunch, and you need to plan accordingly—story time, free choice, movies, or the like—nothing that is academic or that requires too much sitting. By the time they reach second grade, most children are "schoolwise" and have the stamina to make it through the day relatively easily.

It is a good idea to remember that young children tire more easily when they are sitting than when they are active. Remember to alternate active activities frequently with those requiring attention on the teacher. A rule of thumb is not to have any whole-class meeting longer than 10 to 15 minutes during the first few weeks of school.

Kindergarten

A first day in kindergarten may be broken up as shown below. The times listed are approximate. Most activities take much longer the first day. Just remember that most kindergartners do not know how to line up, how to go to a group, how to find the bathroom, and so on. You need to be prepared to have a lot of patience.

20 Minutes: Greeting and Free Choice

Have name tags laid out on a table near the door. Have simple activities on the rest of the tables (e.g., puzzles, Play-Doh, books, paper and crayons, stencils). Station yourself by the door to greet the students and their parents. Quickly have each student find his or her name tag, then show the student his or her cubby and direct him or her to find something to do on one of the tables. Send the parent with the child, making it clear that at your signal parents are to leave. (Your aide or coteacher should be in charge of the tables, making sure to direct students to only those activities you have put out.)

This opening should last about 20 minutes. Try to have parents leave before you clean up the activities. (In subsequent years you may want parents to stay as long as they wish, but it is recommended that in your first year you will want to establish yourself with your students without an audience. This is a touchy situation that you will have to play by ear. Just remember that often a crier or clinger will be fine once the parent leaves.)

15 Minutes: Whole-Group Circle

After 20 minutes, make your freeze-and-listen signal. This will be the first time, so it may take some time and the cooperation and help of all the adults in the room to pull off this transition. Make sure the adults are stationed throughout the room and that they freeze and listen in a very pointed way and help those students near them to freeze as well when you make the signal. *Praise* those who freeze. With the adults' help, have the students clean up and then come to the whole-group area. You should be at the whole-group area, directing students where to sit. If you have marked the area with tape, this shouldn't be too difficult.

Once the majority of the students are with you, start a fingerplay. Just do it—don't try to teach it the first time through. A good one to do would be "Five Little Monkeys Jumping on the Bed" because it's a counting down fingerplay and will last long enough that everyone will be able to join you by the time you finish.

Now you can introduce all the adults in the room, including yourself. Do a short name song or chant.

Do the freeze-and-listen modeling lesson described in Chapter 2.

Practice several more fingerplays or songs: "Open Them, Shut Them," "Johnny Works With One Hammer," "Abranlas, Ciérranlas," or others.

Talk about bathroom procedures—who can go and when, what the system is, and so on.

Introduce the idea of small-group time. If you have color coded the necklace name tags with different colors of yarn or different shapes, you can have your students go to their groups according to that system. If not, just send them as they are grouped on the rug. For bilingual classes, you may have to be a bit more selective because of language, but if your activity doesn't depend a lot on language, heterogeneous groups are fine.

30 Minutes: Small-Group Teacher-/Aide-Directed Activities

Plan to divide your students into as many groups as you have adults to supervise. Each group may do the same activity, but an adult will be with each group. Hopefully, you will have at least three adults.

You want to have this activity produce something the student can take home that day. It should also be designed to give you an opportunity to observe such skills as cutting, name writing, and pencil holding in a small-group setting. Note any real problem areas—remember, you are not assessing each child, just getting a general feel. Provide each adult with a clipboard and checklist to note any problem areas.

Select a short book for each adult to read or a poem having to do with what you're making. A simple cut-and-paste project is best, using a precut shape to make a picture. For example, a big circle and a smaller circle can make a cat. Leave some creativity for the child. He or she could add the ears, face, and background for the picture. The finished products shouldn't all look the same.

The adults should talk about and model where to get supplies, how to use them, how to clean up, where to put the finished products, and so on. They should also model how to do the project in a step-by-step fashion: "First you get a big circle." Wait until everyone has the big circle. "Now you paste it at the bottom of the paper like this." The adult models on his or her paper, and so on. Instruct the adults to keep students at their centers until you give the freeze-and-listen signal. This is where you use those preselected books to read.

At the end of the activity, you should make your freeze-and-listen signal, wait until everyone has frozen, and then give the next direction. Praise those freezing—you can even go over to someone and point out how frozen he or she is. Instruct students to clean up and then come to the whole-group meeting area.

15 Minutes: Whole Group Circle

Again do a fingerplay or two to settle students. Repeating the same ones you did earlier is a good idea.

Do the calendar routine (see Chapter 2). On the first day you might just model this activity, instead of having a student help you. See Chapter 5 for a song to sing about the days of the week.

Your students will be ready for a recess about now. The goal of this circle time is to talk about the procedures for recess. Include the "how to's" of lining up, where the children may play and where they may not, bathroom policy, what the signal will be to come in, and what the procedure will be for lining up. Some kindergartens have a snack at this time. If that is the case for your class, you will need to discuss snack routine as well.

Dismiss students a few at a time according to some criterion—all those wearing blue, all those with a bear name tag, and so on. Model how one should get in line and how to wait until all are ready to walk outside.

10-15 Minutes: Recess

Decide ahead of time who will supervise outside activities and who will set up inside activities. Some schools require that a certificated person be on the yard at all times with students. If this is so, either you or your cooperating teacher will need to be outside. If not, your aide could cover this recess while you set up.

Following the recess and another short whole-group session, you will want to have a free-choice activity time. That means your tables need to be set up with what the students can choose. Use recess time to get this set up. Put out some of the same activities you had available in the morning—puzzles and so on—plus open the playhouse, put out big blocks, and have one or two simple art projects. Have at least eight choices. For example, in one free-choice period you might have available the playhouse, blocks, puzzles, colored markers for drawing, stencils, easel painting, pegboards, Legos, Play-Doh, and adult-directed art activities, such as watercolors or a cut-and-paste project. Remember, the students will self-select these activities, so some thought needs to be given to how many students can be in each area and how that will be determined. Self-selection training will be done at a whole-group session after recess.

15 Minutes: Whole-Group Story and Music

When students have returned from outside, read them one or two short stories. You might introduce a song that has a follow-up activity during free choice (e.g., "Wheels on the Bus," or "Five Little Monkeys" with a monkey follow-up).

30 Minutes: Free Choice

Explain the choices available. Students should be encouraged to stick with a project until completion. Reinforce that everyone must clean up before moving to another area. State how many students can be at each activity at any one time (if you provide enough choices, you shouldn't have problems).

Excuse the students to make their choices in an orderly fashion; for example, you might have all students wearing green socks line up first. Your aide and, if possible, your cooperating teacher should be sitting at their activities. Some students are drawn to adults. You should be free to roam, questioning students, reminding them to clean up before they move on, redirecting students, and so on.

Take some time yourself to get to know a few students individually. Get down on their level and talk to them about what they are doing and why. Try to identify any students who are having a difficult time making choices and sticking with them. Those are students you may have to conference with in the future before sending them to free choice. Most of all, try to enjoy this part of the day.

10 Minutes: Cleanup

Make your freeze-and-listen signal. Reinforce freezing again in an exaggerated way. (Down the line, freezing will become a problem if students feel that the only time you make the signal is for cleanup. Therefore, it is important to make freezing an integral part of the signal.)

When you have all students' attention, explain cleanup. Each adult should work with those students close to him or her to help clean up. Students should be instructed to come to the circle only after they have cleaned up.

You might want to put on a soothing record as students begin to come to the circle. Remember to use a calm and quiet voice; this will also help calm the transition. Again, start a fingerplay or song when you have most of the group.

10-15 Minutes: Whole-Group Circle Time

Read another short book or share the products of the free-choice time. Do another song or two. If you feel the students are antsy, you may want to take another short recess. This will depend on your group, and usually you would want to eliminate this recess as the year goes on.

20 Minutes: Tour of the School

If you don't take a recess, you might want to take a tour of the school. This is best done in small groups, using the three adults you had during group time, if possible. The tour should include the office, the cafeteria, the big playground, the bathrooms outside the kindergarten room, the library, and any other places unique to your school. Alert personnel in these areas as to the approximate time you will be coming, and ask them to be prepared to give a short presentation of what happens in that place. Have a different route for each group (e.g., your group might start in the office, your aide's in the library, and your coteacher's in the cafeteria).

You may not get around to giving the school tour on the first day of school, but try to fit it in sometime during the first week. If you elect not to do the tour, the following is an alternate activity.

30 Minutes: Introduction of Math Manipulatives

Do a quick whole-group lesson such as rhythmic clapping or a group counting song or chant.

Divide your class in half. Have one of the halves divide in half again, to work with your aide and coteacher with puzzles at one table and books or coloring at another. You will be responsible for introducing a math manipulative (e.g., Unifix cubes, pattern blocks) to half the group for 10 minutes and then you will switch with those at the tables. See the first chapter of *Mathematics Their Way*, by Mary Baratta-Lorton, for further explanation of this process (for publication details on this and other books mentioned in this volume, see Chapter 8).

During the introduction of the math manipulative, be sure to cover the proper use of the material and the rule that what you make is yours. Others should ask permission to work with you, even during cleanup.

15 Minutes: Closing

You've almost made it. Gather students back at the circle for a recap of the day. Some teachers do a daily "language experience newspaper" at this time to review what has happened. Some share selected products from the day. Whatever you choose, make this a calming culmination of a busy time.

During the first week, allow time for students to get bus tags pinned on and plenty of time to be at the bus loading area, especially if your students will be riding the buses with older students.

The general plan outlined above could be used daily for the first week (minus the tour of the school, of course). Try to set your first day and week as closely as possible to what your schedule will be for the year. To reiterate, students like and need routine. The sooner your students learn the routines, the sooner your energy can be spent on planning exciting curriculum.

First Grade

A first day in first grade would follow a combination of activities, similar to those used in kindergarten. A helpful hint about the first week is that your language arts time should be based on literature—meaning both books and poetry or chants—and can be the basis of whole-class projects. Math time should be devoted to free exploration and introduction of the manipulatives you will use during the year—pattern blocks, Unifix cubes, beans, geoboards, wooden cubes, and so on. See the first chapter of *Mathematics Their Way* for further explanation.

First grade should continue to have a self-selected free-choice time at some point during the day, with open-ended activities similar to those used in kindergarten (blocks, puzzles, markers, clay, books, listening center, and so on).

During the first month, introduce art media the students will be using throughout the year in a directed manner (e.g., watercolors, chalk, cut and paste, tempera paint). Students should be allowed to explore freely with these materials once they have been taught their proper use.

If you are a first-grade teacher, read the above kindergarten first day, and then look at the following schedule for the first day of first grade:

20 Minutes: Greeting and Free Choice

* See the greeting plan for kindergarten.

20 Minutes: Whole Group on the Floor

* Do introductions; play one of the name games described in Chapter 4.
* Give the freeze-and-listen lesson.
* Introduce the language arts activity.

30 Minutes: Language Arts Activity

* Depending on the availability of an aide at this time, do this activity as a whole-group "following directions" activity, or divide the class into two groups.

10 Minutes: Review Cleanup and Recess Procedures

- Freeze and listen, clean up the language arts project, and sit at desks/tables or on the floor, depending on your room arrangement.
- Discuss recess rules, lining-up rules, and what to do when the bell rings.

20 Minutes: Whole Group

- Sing a song, do a fingerplay.
- Conduct the calendar routine.

20 Minutes: Whole-Group Math Activity

- Do a counting game or song, such as "Cookie Jar?" using numeral cards instead of names.
- Introduce rhythmic clapping, using students' names.
- As an alternative to rhythmic clapping, make a graph of bus routes.

30 Minutes: Math Manipulative Introduction/Free Exploration

- See the kindergarten activities explanation, above.

10 Minutes: Cleanup

- Review the freeze-and-listen procedure, then clean up and come to the floor.

20 Minutes: Prepare for Lunch

- Review what students learned during math.
- Do rhythmic clapping, using student names.
- Talk about lunch procedures, cafeteria rules, and recess rules.
- Walk to lunch.

Lunch

15 Minutes: Story Time

- Have available at least two participation-type books (e.g., *Brown Bear, Brown Bear*; *Rosie's Walk*; or *El Oso Más Elegante*). Big Books would be great, but they are not totally necessary.

- Preview the book in L1 (that day or week's first language; see the section on bilingual strategies in Chapter 2) if you have a bilingual class.
- Encourage student participation, body movements, role playing.
- Read the books at least twice.
- Consider developing a simple follow-up activity to have available at free-choice time.

30 Minutes: Free-Choice Time

- During lunch, set up activities from which the students may choose. Using tubs or boxes color coded to labels in your room will facilitate passing out these activities.
- Quickly tell the students what is available and how many can be at each center. You may not have another adult to supervise an activity, so don't plan anything students cannot do by themselves. You want to be free to roam and observe. Choosing simple activities is best.
- Review your freeze-and-listen signal before you excuse students to free choice.
- Excuse in an orderly fashion; for example, "All those wearing blue may choose," or "Who would like to be at the Legos?" (Hint: Offer the least desirable choice first.)

10 Minutes: Cleanup

- Give the freeze-and-listen signal. Explain cleanup, reinforcing where things go. Praise. Meet at the floor area.

20 Minutes: Review, Sharing of Day

- Have a student share what he or she did at free choice. You might consider putting this sharing up on a language experience chart.
- Sing a song, do a fingerplay, reread one of the participation books.

15 Minutes: Prepare to Go Home

- Pass out bus tags, pass out any papers.
- Review bus procedures.
- Line up and walk to the bus.

THE FIRST DAY OF SCHOOL, INTERMEDIATE GRADES

All of the activities referred to below are described in detail in Chapter 4. Also see Chapter 2 for sample procedural charts for each learning situation.

Before Students Arrive

Have some games and puzzles available (two to five) at a back table for those students who come to school early the first day. Have the Wiggly Line ditto on desks (see Chapter 4). Have a bulletin board ready so you can put the finished Wiggly Line drawings and stories up. *Stand at the door* to greet your students.

Seating Arrangements

You can set up a seating chart ahead of time, let students self-select seats, or allow them to select according to categories. For example, you may set the guideline that two boys and two girls need to sit at each desk cluster.

Activities for the Day

20-30 Minutes: Wiggly Line

Students come in and begin working on Wiggly Line immediately. Explain that you want each student to create a picture and write a story about it, using the line on the paper. As students finish their pictures and stories, have them bring them to you. Put them up immediately on the prepared bulletin board. As each student finishes, have him or her pick up an information card (index card) and print on it his or her name, address, and phone number, as well as the name(s) of his or her guardian(s). Have an example on the board.

Attention Signal

Decide how you want to get the students' attention (e.g., raise your hand, speak, ring a bell). Use this attention-getting signal and wait until you have everyone looking at you. Usually the first morning this is not a problem, but if it is, praise those who are giving attention while stating the behavior you are waiting for: "Thank you, Mary. Thank you, Juan, for stopping and looking up at me." When you have everyone's attention, praise them all and restate the behavior that you are praising them for: "Great, everyone has stopped working and is looking at me. This is exactly what I want you to do when I give the attention signal."

10 Minutes: Introductions

Introduce yourself to your students. Let them know a little bit about who you are. Ask questions about their anticipation for the first day. Use humor! (If your class comes in all together, you may do this first.)

40 Minutes: Circle Time

Tell students where to put their belongings (e.g., coats on hangers, supplies in desks). Explain, "Now we're going to do an activity where you'll need to sit on the floor." Show the students the parameters of your circle, and tell them how you want them to move to the rug area (circle) for this activity. Call categories to have students move to the rug area (e.g., all those wearing red, all those with a birthday in January). Students should put their belongings wherever you need them to on their way to the circle. Use one of the name games from Chapter 4.

10 Minutes: Before-Recess Transition Procedures

Leaving and entering the room. Do they wait to be dismissed by row, by categories you name, by the team that is ready? Will they line up? Where will they line up? Is there a line leader? What behavior is expected in line?

Snack procedures. Where should they eat?

Ball or equipment checkout procedures. Label equipment with your name and room number. Put a different letter on each piece of equipment. Student monitors can check out equipment using these letters.

Choosing books for silent reading. Explain to the students that before they go to recess they are to choose silent reading books to have on their desks when they come in from recess. (Have a box of books at each table for them to choose from.) Explain that when they come in from recess they will sit down and begin reading these books; show them the silent reading procedure chart (see Chapter 2).

20 Minutes: Silent Reading

Meet students at their line before they come in, and praise their positive behavior. If there were any problems during recess, reiterate the expected behavior. Remind students to enter the room with no talking and begin immediately to read silently. Pick up your own book and model that behavior.

40 Minutes: Attention Signal, Class Discussion

Give your attention-getting signal, and praise positive responses. State the expected behavior, for example, "Great job of looking at me right away. Now please put your books in your desk and give me your attention; we're going to have a class discussion." Explain procedures for a class discussion: Stay seated at your desk, raise your hand when you want to speak, listen while others speak, and so on. Now explain the activity, Please . . . Please Don't . . . (see Chapter 4).

During the remaining time until lunch, do finish-up work. Explain the procedures for independent work. Have students finish their Wiggly Line stories, name tags, information cards, and so on.

5-10 Minutes: Before Lunch

Go over lunch procedures:

- Where do they eat? Are there special rules there?
- Review the playground rules.
- Review procedures for returning to class after lunch.

20 to 30 Minutes: Read Aloud

See the list of suggested books for reading aloud in Chapter 8. Explain the procedures for read-alouds, as discussed in Chapter 2.

10 to 15 Minutes: Jobs

Tell the students about the classroom jobs you have assigned, or brainstorm as a class the jobs that need to be done (see the jobs chart and discussion in Chapter 2). Show and explain the system you will use to rotate jobs. Role-play how one does each job.

5 Minutes: Before P.E.

Explain procedures for outside behavior, where to meet, how to get there, a signal for stopping, and so on.

20 Minutes: P.E.

Play Knots, the Lap Game, or any other P.E. games you choose (see Chapter 4 for ideas). Explain the procedures for returning to class: Are students allowed to run? Should they walk? May they get drinks of water? May they talk in the hallways? Provide an incentive for correct behavior, such as, "I'm looking for line leaders for next week. I'll choose those who can follow directions entering and leaving the room."

15 Minutes: Homework

Have students sit at their desks while you explain the homework assignment. Give the assignment to write a short essay titled "Who Lives at My House." Say, "I want to know what your household is like. Describe all the people who live in your house. I want to know as much as you can tell me about them. When you bring the homework in tomorrow, it goes in the red basket by the door. I expect you to bring your homework every day." Give each student a notepad of recycled paper to write down the homework assignment, and then walk around the room to make sure everyone has copied the day's assignment. (See Chapter 4 for more homework ideas.)

Sponge Activity

If there is extra time, use one of the sponge activities described in Chapter 4 or sing the "Name Song" (see Chapter 5).

10 Minutes: Before Dismissal

Have students perform their assigned jobs and have the class evaluate the work done. Ask questions such as, "How does the library corner look?" "Is the floor clean?"

Dismissal

Review bus rules or the rules for walking home. Remind students what is expected in the morning. Stand at the door and say something pleasant to students as they leave. Use their names as much as possible.

4 Activities for the First Month

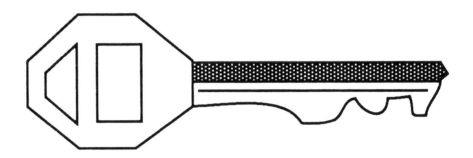

Activities for the first month of school should build self-esteem, foster classroom unity, allow you and your students to get acquainted, and generate student excitement about being in your classroom.

CHAPTER CONTENTS

PLANNING GUIDE FOR THE FIRST MONTH OF SCHOOL

The handwritten calendar shown on the next page gives you an overview of how you might plan your activities during the first month of school. It shows when to begin ongoing activities and suggests an order for presenting the daily activities.

The next few pages give sample lesson plans for the first three to four weeks. We provide a very detailed plan for the first week in kindergarten, using the theme of bears (see page 55). Modifications for the first grade follow, as do suggestions for continuing routines and new material for the second, third, and fourth weeks.

Sample plans are also included for the first three weeks in grades 2 through 5. Note that activities are quite different in those grades, to take into account increasing levels of reading ability.

First Week of First Grade

First grade will be very similar to kindergarten. Follow the general plan outlined for kindergarten. Use the schedule on page 54 and adjust the time slots to fit the kindergarten plan.

8:15 - 8:45	opening
8:45 - 9:45	literacy—whole-group shared reading
9:45-10:00	recess
10:00-10:45	small-group literacy lessons
10:45-11:25	math
11:30-12:15	lunch
12:15-12:45	story time; introduction of DEAR time
1:00 - 3:00	activity time
1:30 - 1:45	closing

Second Week of School, Kindergarten/First Grade (Theme: Bears, Teddy Bears)

You will want to continue the following routines.

Opening

Continue to take roll, focusing on the children's learning each others' names.

Continue to introduce fingerplays and songs, and review literature and songs daily. Put the most familiar song on a large chart, and use it to develop literacy skills.

Introduce, model, and role-play the use of the independent center. See the following section on literacy.

KINDERGARTEN   THEME: BEARS

FIRST WEEK OF SCHOOL

TIME	MONDAY	TUESDAY	WEDNESDAY	THURSDAY	FRIDAY
8:15-8:45 Opening	•Greet children/parents •Free choice •8:30: Fingerplay, roll, introductions	•Roll: Greet by name •Fingerplay •Review: The Best Dressed Bear	•Roll: Roll a ball to each child while saying name •Teach Good Day/Buenos Dias; Review lit & poems	•Roll: Each stand as name is said. Everyone says Good Morning Buenos Dias___ •Review	•Roll: Show name card as you say name. •Review fingerplays/lit
8:45-9:15 Literacy	Form 3-4 groups w/yarn necklaces. Each group: Literature: Read: The Best Dressed Bear/El Oso Más Elegante Activity: Trace, color, cut out bear Focus: Care of books: listening behavior	Form groups again. Literature: Read: The Three Bears/Los Tres Osos Activity: Cut 3 Os with mama, papa and baby bears pictured. Paste on Os of corresponding size. Focus: Pasting, writing name on papers	Form groups again: Literature: Read: Brown Bear/Oso Café Activity: Remove a common object from feely box. Child names color and places object on animal from story. Focus: Taking turns, helping others	Forms groups again: Literature: Read Corduroy Activity: Directed draw bear. Children add details from story. Orally retell the story from the pictures. Focus: Listening to others, follow directions	•Form groups again •Introduce journals •Activity: Mini-lesson on what it means to write and be an author. Children date, draw pic and write on self selected topic. Focus: Material storage and use
9:15-9:30 Circle Time	•Model calendar routine with aide as "helper" •Freeze & listen	•Model calendar routine with you as "helper" •Teach Three Bears Chant	•Choose a helper •Calendar routine •Chant Brown Bear	•Choose helper •Calendar routine •Three Bears Chant	•Choose helper •Calendar routine •Review If You're Happy
9:30-9:45 Recess	•Follow the leader outside to explain rules	Same as Mon.	Free Play	Free Play	Free play
9:45-10:00 Circle time	•Story •Teach Five Bears Jumping on the bed •Intro free choice	•Story •Review Three Bears Chant/5 Bears Jumping	•Story •Review Brown Bear Chant	•Story •Teach: If You're Happy and You Know It/Si feliz..	•Story •Make a real graph of favorite book from M-Th
10:00-10:40 Activity Time	activities in 3 sm. grps: -Writing Center -Art Center -Manipulatives	•Rotate groups from Mon. •Intro the same activities to a different group •Freeze/model clean up procedures	•Rotate groups from Tues. •Intro same activities to last group •Freeze/model clean up procedures	•Intro to whole group: -Playdough-Puzzles •All self select activities from available choices •Freeze/Clean Up may need this break.	•Intro to whole group Playhouse and blocks. •All self select activities from available choices •Freeze/Clean Up
10:40-10:50 Movement/Recess	This recess may	disappear after a couple	weeks, but initially you		
10:50-11:20 Math	Refer to Math Their Way Chap. 1 •Intro unifix cubes to •Others books, coloring Flip groups after 15 min.	•Intro pattern blocks to half. •Others choose from books, coloring or unifix Flip groups after 15 min.	•Intro Geoboards to half •Others choose from pattern blocks or unifix	•Intro tubbing •Children choose from unifix, pattern blocks or geoboards	•Review tubbing •Children choose from pattern blocks, unifix or geoboards
11:20-11:35 Closing	•Bus tags •Review day	•Bus tags •Review day	•Bus tags •Review day	•Bus tags •Review day	•Bus tags •Review day

SEPTEMBER PLANNING GUIDE

MON.	TUES.	WED.	THURS.	FRI.
- Wiggly Line - Action Names - Procedures for recess - Silent reading - Please, Please Don't - Read Aloud - Brainstorm jobs - P.E.	- Beginning the day - journals - Initial Adjective Names - Please, Please Don't (day 2) - silent reading - Partner Introductions - Read Aloud - Me pictures - P.E.	- Beginning the day - journals - Math challenges - The Class Age - silent reading - Name Song - Find Someone Who... - Read Aloud - Me pictures - P.E pictures	- Beginning the day - journals - Math challenges - People Measuring - silent reading - Appreciation Words - Positive Adjectives - Read Aloud - Partner Draw - P.E.	- Beginning the day - journals - Math challenges - Graphing - silent reading - What I Think About Writing - shields - classmeeting - clean desks and room - Free Play P.E.
- Daily Activities — Math Computation check	Continue (beginning the day, journals, math challenges, silent reading, and read aloud)			
- Math Computation check - Letter - Name Bingo - Literature Logs - Shields (day 2) - Silhouette Murals - P.E.	- Broken Circles - Literature Logs - Group definition of Cooperation - Silhouette Murals/ free draw - P.E.	- Begin School Math Program - Literature Logs - Famous Quotes - Name scramble I - Graffitti Boards - P.E.	- School Math Program - Literature Logs - Student Self-Assess. - Name scramble II - Graffitti Boards - P.E.	- School Math Program - Literature Logs - Paired Interviews - classmeeting/Garfunkle Story - clean desks and room - Free Play P.E.
- Daily Activities	Continue (beginning the day, journals, literature logs, read a loud) On-going Reading, Math and P.E programs. continue			
- Begin School Reading Program			- Raisin Estimation	- Raisin Estimation - classmeeting - clean desks and room - Free Play P.E.
- Know Your Classmate	- Cheerios	- Conflict Resolution	- Conflict Resolution	
- Continue established daily routines - Continue on-going programs - Begin social Studies / Science		thematic program		

Literacy

When planning literacy activities, it is helpful to choose a book to be the focus of each lesson. The follow-up activity can relate to the book and, in these first few weeks of school, a focus behavior should be part of the lesson.

Plan four activities for the week. Three activities should be supervised by adults, typically yourself, your aide, and your cooperating teacher; the fourth will be an independent center. Spend some time during your opening each day to introduce and model appropriate behavior at the independent center. Each activity should last for the 30-minute period. Divide your class into four heterogeneous groups. Rotate groups through the activities at the rate of one per day. It is helpful to minimize the number of transitions the children have to make. At each table, provide a tub of books for the children to look at if they finish the activity early.

Suggested literacy activities for a teddy bear theme include the following:

- *Read a teddy bear book.* Stop at an appropriate point, and tell the children the teddy bear is lost and the class has to find it. Use this as an introduction to a tour of the school. Make arrangements ahead of time with the office, cafeteria, and custodial staff. Find the teddy bear in the principal's office. If there is time, have the group dictate a language experience story about the tour.

- *Teach "Teddy Bear, Teddy Bear, Turn Around."* Have the children act out the rhyme, then brainstorm other actions a teddy bear could do. Have each child draw a picture of a teddy bear doing another action. An adult can write the words for the actions, and the pages can be bound to make a group book.

- *Journals.* Journals will become a regular group activity. Model again what it means to write in a journal, and suggest the children write about teddy bears. For kindergarten, it will be important to respond in writing to each child's entry, so plan for a sponge activity to give you enough time to respond (see the section on sponge activities, below). A good sponge for the journal center would be to provide other writing materials—chalkboards, different size paper and writing implements, magnetic letters—from which the children can choose after they finish writing in their journals and are waiting for you to respond.

- *Independent center.* Provide Play-Doh, puzzles and books about teddy bears, and other manipulatives for this group of children to explore independently. Use materials that you have introduced during free-choice time the week before. If possible, get a cross-age tutor to monitor this center.

On Friday, plan a whole-group activity. For example, show the video of *Corduroy.* Then plan a simple art or cooking project as a follow-up to the video.

Circle Time

Continue to stress the calendar routine.

Develop a clear system for choosing your helper of the day.

Review the songs and poems you have already introduced.

Recess

Assess how the children are following the rules. Continue to model and review yard rules.

Circle Time

You may want to use this time for a story, and then introduce Drop Everything and Read (DEAR) time (see the discussion of silent reading in Chapter 2).

Activity Time

As you add choices to this time, introduce and model each to the whole class. Explain the procedures, rules, and cleanup for each activity.

Assess the children's abilities to make choices. Focus on those children having difficulty. Spend some time helping them make and stick with choices.

Second Recess

Evaluate whether the children seem to need a break at this time. You may decide to do a more structured movement activity rather than a free-play recess. For example:

- Explore the movement records available. Those by Hap Palmer, Ella Jenkins, Greg and Steve, and José Luis Orozco, for instance, might be helpful. Use these to get ideas for activities you could do.
- Teach simple circle games, such as Duck, Duck, Goose or Sally Go Round the Sun.

Math

Begin each math time with a whole-group lesson. For the teddy bear theme, consider asking the children to bring in teddy bears, or you can make a collection. Use this collection to do the following whole-group lessons:

- Count the bears.
- Sort and classify the bears (color, dressed/not dressed, and so on).
- Seriate the bears by size.
- Make patterns with the bears.
- Make a real graph of the bears (by color, size, and the like).

Continue to follow the procedures for introducing new math manipulatives.

Continue modeling the tubbing procedures outlined in *Mathematics Their Way*, Chapter 1.

Closing

Bus tags may still be important this second week. Check with the bus drivers.

Review each day's activities and events. You might consider beginning a class newspaper. Have the children dictate the events from the day while you write them on chart paper. Use this list the next day to remind the children what they have done.

Third and Fourth Weeks
(Possible Themes: Real Bears/
Bears in Literature)

Opening

Continue the same routines. Use this time as well to do any whole-group theme-related lessons.

Literacy

You are well on your way now. With the basic structure of time slots you have created in the first two weeks, your planning is streamlined. The third week's theme could be real bears. Develop activities that develop the children's interest in bear facts, types of bears, and so on. In the fourth week of the bear themes you could continue to study real bears or look at more bears in literature.

Circle Time

Continue with the calendar routine. Begin making charts of well-known songs and poems. Use these to develop children's sense of themselves as readers.

Recess

Assess whether this break is long enough, whether you need to add more structure, who needs help finding someone to play with, and so on.

Circle Time

Continue to read aloud to the children at this time. Be consistent about the procedures for DEAR time.

Activity Time

Continue some of the same activities from the first two weeks. Some of these choices may be available all year.

Remember to introduce and model any new activity thoroughly before allowing it to become a choice.

Math

Continue with a whole-group lesson related to your theme at the beginning of the math period.

Continue free-exploration tubbing.

Closing

You may wish to begin a class newspaper at this time. Have the children dictate important events from the day while you write them out on chart paper.

First Weeks of Grades 2-5

Activities for grades 2-5 will be quite distinct from K-1 in the first weeks of school. Use the following schedule as a general guide (you'll want to transfer this to a weekly calendar):

8:30 - 9:00	opening
9:00-10:00	math
10:00-10:20	recess
10:20-10:40	silent reading
10:40-12:00	language arts
12:00-12:44	lunch
12:45 - 1:05	reading aloud
1:05 - 2:15	social studies
2:15 - 2:30	closing

Activity Suggestions: First Week

- *Opening:* Wiggly Line worksheet, journals.
- *Math:* Name games, Please . . . Please Don't . . . (Day 2), math challenges, the class age, People Measuring, graphing. (On Day 1, go over procedures for recess just prior to 10:00.)
- *Language arts:* Please . . . Please Don't . . . (Day 1), Partner Introductions, sponge activities, name games ("Name Song"), Find Someone Who . . . worksheet, Appreciation Words, Positive Adjectives, What I Think About Writing worksheet, Shields. (On Day 1, go over procedures for lunch just prior to 12:00; on Day 2, give reminders about lunch procedures.)
- *Reading aloud:* Select an appropriate grade-level book from the resources listed in Chapter 8 of this volume.
- *Social studies:* Brainstorm classroom jobs, P.E. (the Lap Game), Me Pictures, P.E. (Knots), partner drawings, P.E. (relays), free-play P.E. (On Day 5, do thorough room and desk cleanups; allow time for free play.)

- *Closing:* Assign homework, clean room, do sponge activities. (On Day 5, pass out student homework to go home and file the rest.)

Activity Suggestions: Second and Third Weeks

- *Opening:* Beginning the day, journals.
- *Math:* Math challenges, math computation check, cooperative triangles, raisin estimation. Begin the school math program in the middle of the second week.
- *Language arts:* Letters, Bingo, literature logs, Group Definition of Cooperation, Famous Quotes, Name Scramble, student self-assessment, Name Scramble II, paired interviews. Begin the school reading program in the third week.
- *Reading aloud:* Select an appropriate grade-level book from the resources listed in Chapter 8 of this volume.
- *Social studies/science/art:* Literature logs, Shields, silhouette murals, P.E., free drawing, Graffiti Boards, Know Your Classmate worksheet, brainstorming using Cheerios, sponge activities (Line-Ups, People Sorting). (On Day 5 of each week, do thorough room and desk cleanups; allow some time for free play.)
- *Closing:* Assign homework, clean room, do sponge activities. (On Day 5, pass out student homework to go home and file the rest.)

ORAL LANGUAGE AND TEAM-/ CLASS-BUILDING ACTIVITIES

APPRECIATION WORDS

MATERIALS: paper, pencils, chart paper (optional)

GROUPING: whole class and teams

APPROXIMATE TIME: 20-30 minutes

DIRECTIONS:

(1) Choose one child who needs to build his or her self-esteem, and write a list of 6-10 words describing that person. Use words that describe his or her special attributes, such as *caring, helpful, a good listener, friendly, good at sports, creative, thoughtful,* and *contributes to class discussions.* Review the procedures for teacher-led discussion.

(2) Have the class guess who the person might be. Write each guess on the board.

(3) After several guesses, tell the class that all their guesses are right in a way, because all of the people they guessed have these characteristics.

(4) Tell them the name of the person you thought of when making the list.

(5) As a class or in teams, brainstorm words of appreciation. It might help if you ask the students to think about particular people. Younger students could think about characters from a book you have read to them. Make a list from the students' suggestions and display it in the room.

EXTENSION: Throughout the year, have the class develop a list of appreciation words for a special student. Record the words on chart paper for the student to take home at the end of the week. Students may also sign the chart or write personal comments and compliments on it before it is taken home. Periodically, discuss words from the list (their meanings, the type of things a person would do to exhibit a particular attribute, and so on) and add a couple of the words to your regular spelling list.

WORDS OF PRAISE: Following is a list of words that might help you with this activity if the class gets stuck. You might also give students the task of alphabetizing these words.

friendly	cheerful
helpful	loyal
responsible	flexible

reliable
generous
thoughtful
caring
humorous
polite
eager
enthusiastic
fair

creative
energetic
outgoing
courageous
resourceful
willing
organized
compassionate
considerate

A list of Spanish words of praise may also be useful:

amistoso
agradable
compasivo
productivo
generoso
beneficioso
intrépido
inventivo
justo
considerado
cortéz
vigoroso
inspirado
flexible

enérgico
interesante
deseoso
comprensivo
selectivo
amable
responsable
habil
entusiasta
alegre
puntual
estudioso
capaz

POSITIVE ADJECTIVES

MATERIALS: tagboard, tape, pencils

GROUPING: whole class

APPROXIMATE TIME: 45 minutes

DIRECTIONS:

(1) As a class, brainstorm a large list of positive adjectives.

(2) Split the class up into cooperative groups or partners, and have students come up with 10 positive adjectives for one another.

(3) As an alternative, you can tape a piece of tagboard with lined paper attached to each person's back. Tell the students that when you give the signal they are to see how many different people's backs they can write positive adjectives on (have them initial the adjectives). A team may sit down as soon as each person on the team has 10 adjectives.

(4) Have students recopy the positive adjectives about themselves, using "I am . . . " or "John says . . . " forms (for example, "I am intelligent," or "Mary thinks I'm fascinating").

CLOSURE: Have a discussion about how the activity made students feel. Ask, "What can we learn from this that will make our class a nicer place to be?"

BINGO

MATERIALS: enough Bingo game sheets for all students (see following page), all students' names written on separate pieces of paper, a bag or other container to put the names in, "prizes"

GROUPING: whole class

APPROXIMATE TIME: 20-30 minutes

DIRECTIONS:

(1) Have paper monitors pass out the Bingo sheets.

(2) Explain the directions and your behavioral expectations. Tell the students, "This activity is a fun way to learn your classmates' names. At the signal, write one name in each box on the Bingo sheet. Do not use any name twice. Try to write as many names as you can from memory. You may use your own name. Then, I will pull a name from this bag. If you have that name on your Bingo sheet, cross it off. When you have five names crossed off in a row, vertically, horizontally, or diagonally, say 'Bingo.' "

(3) Check for the students' understanding of the directions, then give the signal to start.

(4) Circulate around the room to prompt students. They should be able to fill in the names on their sheets in 5-10 minutes, depending on the grade level. For younger students: (a) Make a game board with fewer boxes, (b) write students' names so that they just need to recognize the beginning sounds, and (c) have students work in pairs.

(5) Give your zero-noise signal and repeat the procedures again if the students begin to call out during the game.

(6) Play until someone says, "Bingo." Verify the names he or she has crossed out with the names you've pulled out of the bag. Continue play until another student has Bingo. Repeat until several students "win."

(7) Give out "prizes" of graham crackers, raisins, popcorn, or the like. Be sure everyone gets a "prize." You might want to give the "winners" a little more. This game is good to play right before recess, so the students can be excused as soon as they get their snacks.

NAME _____

Bingo

		FREE		

CONFLICT RESOLUTION: I MESSAGES

MATERIALS: none

GROUPING: cooperative groups of four

APPROXIMATE TIME: 60 minutes

DIRECTIONS:

(1) Tell your students you'll be working on skits in which they'll be practicing "I messages." Give sample "I messages," such as "I can't think with a lot of noise."

(2) Act out the following skit for the class:

First person: "Jane's hogging the ball. She won't let me play."

Second person: "You're too dumb to play. You don't even know how to play the game. You're a tattletale." (Runs off to join other friends.)

(3) Talk about what happened and the kind of message it was. ("You message," blaming, didn't tell how they felt, or what they needed from the other person. No compromise happened.)

(4) Ask what could have been said instead. Ask, "How can we give better 'I messages.'?" Generate ideas. Have two students act out a better way to resolve the conflict.

(5) Generate a list of things that make students angry. List them on the board.

(6) Divide the class into groups of four. Tell them that each group needs to create a skit in which one person gets angry at the other. Two students from the group will act out the skit with "you messages," and then the other two students will reenact the skit with "I messages" and compromise.

(7) Explain procedures—where you want students to work, the acceptable noise level, and so on. Discuss how the groups might choose the characters for their skits fairly. Give the groups 10-15 minutes to work on their skits.

(8) Bring the students back to their seats and have each group perform its two skits.

CLOSURE: Ask, "What did the groups do differently in the second skits? What did you learn today about resolving conflicts? How can practicing this help our class?"

THE GARFUNKLE STORY

MATERIALS: one large basic paper doll made of construction paper

GROUPING: whole class

APPROXIMATE TIME: 20 minutes

DIRECTIONS:

(1) Hold up a paper doll in front of the class and introduce him as Garfunkle. Explain about a very tough day in his life: He got up late, his mother yelled at him, he spilled his breakfast, he missed his bus or got a bus citation, and on and on, using examples the kids can relate to in your school. It is particularly good to use things you've seen happen in the class. With each negative incident, fold a little part of Garfunkle's body to make the doll shorter, and explain how he felt bad and that made him feel smaller. Keep folding in the parts as he gets smaller and smaller. Have him do something such as tease someone or hit someone to try to feel bigger but instead he gets in trouble and feels even smaller. When you get to the end of your story, Garfunkle should be all folded up.

(2) Talk with the class about how it feels at times like that. Ask how many of them have felt that way at times. Brainstorm ways that the kids in Garfunkle's class could make him feel better. Write them on the board.

(3) Continue the story, using the ideas the class came up with, opening up Garfunkle with each positive experience until he is whole again. Talk about how you have Garfunkles in the class every day.

CLOSURE: Ask, "How can this story help make our class better?"

FOLLOW-UP: Copy the brainstormed list and post it with Garfunkle to remind students of the kinds of things they can do to help each other feel good and whole.

GROUP DEFINITION OF COOPERATION

MATERIALS: large pieces of paper, crayons or markers, writing paper, pencils

GROUPING: cooperative groups of three or four

APPROXIMATE TIME: 45-60 minutes

DIRECTIONS:

(1) Students in cooperative groups number off 1-3 or 1-4, depending on group size. Give each number a job: recorder, reporter, timekeeper, "gopher" (the recorder writes down the group's ideas and final definition, the reporter reports the group's ideas to the class, the timekeeper keeps track of the group's 5 minutes for discussion, and the gopher gets the paper and pencils the group needs).

(2) Tell students that each group will be coming up with a definition of cooperation. All group members must participate and come to consensus on the definition.

(3) Give each group a large piece of paper to draw a mural that reflects the group's definition. Discuss cooperation and involvement of every student in the group. Give approximately 30 minutes for the drawing.

(4) Have the reporters share their groups' definitions of cooperation and their murals.

CLOSURE: Ask students, "How will cooperation help our class this year? What kinds of things can students do to show cooperation—what does cooperation look like and sound like?" Ask each student to tell his or her group one thing he or she liked about the way the group worked today or have individual students write or tell one thing they liked about their own behavior and one thing they can improve.

KNOW YOUR CLASSMATES

MATERIALS: enough teacher-made worksheets for all students, pencils

GROUPING: whole class

APPROXIMATE TIME: 30 minutes

DIRECTIONS:

(1) Make your own worksheet with the blank shown on page 72, or use the one shown on page 71.

(2) Have paper monitors pass out the worksheets.

(3) Explain the directions: "To get the answers to these questions you must walk around the room and talk to every classmate. Being accurate is better than being quick. You'll have about 20 minutes." (The amount of time is up to you. Younger students may need more time or fewer questions.)

(4) Give the signal to begin. Circulate around the room, helping, encouraging, keeping students on task, praising work completed, and/or doing a worksheet yourself.

(5) Use your zero-noise signal to indicate when time is up. Have everyone return to his or her seat.

(6) Go over each question on the worksheet, asking for a show of hands. For example: "Raise your hand if you have more than two pets." "Raise your hand if you have more than four pets." Keep asking questions until you find the student with the most pets, and then ask what types of pets he or she has. The objective of this activity is to help students to get to know their classmates and learn about the differences and similarities among them.

CLOSURE: Ask, "Did anyone learn something about a classmate they didn't know before? What?" Be ready to volunteer what you learned about someone, or point out a similarity you learned through this activity.

Shield

something I do well	something special about my family
algo que puedo hacer bien	algo especial acerca de mi familia
something I like to do with my friends	something my family does together
algo que me gusta hacer con mis amigos	algo que mi familia hace cuando nos juntamos
a four-word phrase describing me	a four-word phrase describing my family
una oración de cuatro palabras que me describe	una oración de cuatro palabras que describe a mi familia

Student's Name

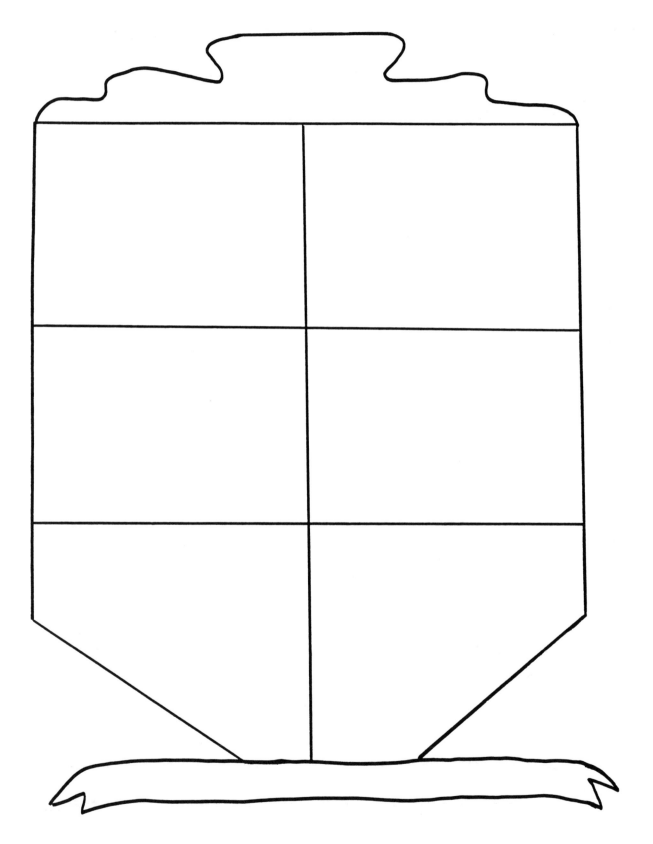

NAME GAMES

——*Action Names*

GROUPING: whole class

APPROXIMATE TIME: 45 minutes

DIRECTIONS:

(1) Have students sit in a circle on the floor.
(2) Going around the circle, each person gives his or her name with an action for each syllable. For example, Josefina would need four syllables. She would say, "Josefina," and then say it again slowly: "Jo"—hits right knee with right hand; "se"—hits left knee with left hand; "fi"—claps hands; "na"—slaps knees with both hands.
(3) Have the whole group repeat the motions, saying the name two times. Then move on to the next person.

——*Initial Adjectives*

GROUPING: cooperative groups

APPROXIMATE TIME: 30 minutes

DIRECTIONS:

(1) In cooperative groups, come up with an adjective to describe each person that starts with that person's initial; for example, Active Abdul or Jumping Jabar.
(2) Have the entire group then create a chant with rhythm motions (clapping, snapping fingers) that includes the names and adjectives of everyone on the team.
(3) Have groups simultaneously share their chants.

——*Name Song*

GROUPING: whole class

APPROXIMATE TIME: Variable

DIRECTIONS: Use the basic name song below and create a song with the names of the students in your class.

Shirley Shirley Bo Birley,
Banana Fana Fo Firley
Fe Fi Mo Mirley, Shirley

——*Name Scramble*

MATERIALS: enough teacher-made worksheets for all students, pencils

GROUPING: whole class at desks

APPROXIMATE TIME: 20 minutes

DIRECTIONS:

(1) Make a worksheet that shows the first names of all students in uppercase letters, with each name scrambled (e.g., Mary might be YARM). Vary the difficulty by (a) writing the first letter in uppercase and the rest of the name in lowercase, (b) underlining the first letter, and (c) posting a class list for the students to refer to.

(2) Explain the directions and behavioral expectations for this activity. Students are to unscramble classmates' names.

(3) Pass out the worksheets.

(4) While the students work on unscrambling the names, move around the class offering help, listening to conversations, encouraging interactions, and keeping students on task.

(5) After 15 minutes, give your zero-noise signal and have students stop working.

(6) Go around the room to "correct" the worksheets. Have one person read the first unscrambled name, then another read the second, and so on. Or do simultaneous sharing, with students calling out their responses. You may have each person whose name has been unscrambled stand up, so students can associate name and face.

CLOSURE: Ask, "Which name was the most difficult to unscramble for you and why?" Also ask, "Why would I want you to do an activity like this?" Finally, ask, "Who can go around the room and name each person?"

——*Name Scramble II*

MATERIALS: pencils, scratch paper, teacher-made name strips printed on 8½ × 2-inch tagboard, with the letters cut apart

GROUPING: whole class at desks, pairs of students, whole class

APPROXIMATE TIME: 45-60 minutes

DIRECTIONS:

(1) Put the cut-up letter pieces for each name in an envelope—one for each name. (To vary the difficulty of this activity, make the pieces larger by cutting between every other letter; make the cuts distinctive, giving visual clues; or place dots on the backs of pieces for last names.)

(2) Explain the directions to the class, including behavioral expectations. Students are to reassemble their classmates' names.

(3) Randomly distribute the envelopes, making sure that no one receives his or her own name.

(4) At your signal, have each student empty his or her envelope and begin to unscramble the mystery name.

(5) Once a student completes the unscrambling task, he or she should find the person whose name is on the strip and "interview" him or her.

(6) Using their own interview questions, interviewers must learn five interesting facts that they will use to introduce the person to the class.

(7) Wander around the room to keep everyone on task and to listen to conversations.

(8) As the students finish, have them check with you to be sure they have completed all parts of the activity. If they have, tell them to write the unscrambled names of the persons they interviewed on the chalkboard. Use this list for the order of introductions. The above steps should take approximately 20 minutes.

(9) Have the students sit at their desks or in a class meeting circle for the introductions.

(10) As the students introduce each other, listen for and note particularly good questions.

CLOSURE:

(1) Discuss the questions and the type of information you would want to know about someone (for instance, "What was one question you thought was particularly good? Why did you like that one? What type of questions help us know more about the person? If you could pick only five questions, which ones would you pick?")

(2) Record the best questions to use as a guide for later in the year to get to know new students.

(3) You might want to videotape or tape-record the introductions to play back at the end of the school year.

PAIRED INTERVIEWS

MATERIALS: paper, pencils

GROUPING: partners

APPROXIMATE TIME: 90 minutes

DIRECTIONS:

(1) Decide as a class on some questions that you would like to ask other people in your class.

(2) Pair up and have partners interview each other and write some notes about their partners.

(3) Have partners introduce each other in cooperative groups.

(4) Have the groups decide on one fact to remember about each person.

(5) Have one person in the group summarize the group introduction by telling the class all the group members' names and the one fact about each person.

CLOSURE: Tell the class how impressed you are with such an interesting group of students. Have them take 3 minutes to write down as many interesting facts as they can remember about their classmates.

SIGNIFICANT OBJECT

MATERIALS: paper, pencils, objects brought from home by students

GROUPING: partners

APPROXIMATE TIME: 90 minutes

DIRECTIONS:

(1) Have each student bring something from home that is very important to him or her, some significant object.

(2) Follow the procedures for paired interviews, having students interview each other to learn about their significant objects.

PARTNER INTRODUCTIONS

MATERIALS: index cards

GROUPING: partners

APPROXIMATE TIME: 60 minutes

DIRECTIONS:

(1) Tell the students that to get acquainted with other students in the class, they'll be doing partner introductions. After answering some questions about themselves, students will partner up and introduce each other to the rest of the class.

(2) Have paper monitors pass out index cards (one per person). In the middle of these cards, have students write their "special interest nicknames"; for example, Adventurous Andrew or Swimming Sandy.

(3) In the upper right-hand corner of the card, have each student write the name of his or her favorite place in the world.

(4) In the bottom left-hand corner of the card, have each student write down something that is important to him or her.

(5) In the top left-hand corner of the card, have each student write something he or she wants to do this year.

(6) In the bottom right-hand corner of the card, have each student write something he or she is good at doing.

(7) Next, have students partner up and share the information about themselves that they have written. Allow approximately 10-15 minutes for this.

(8) Ask for partner volunteers to introduce each other. Encourage students to tell the audience about their partners without reading their cards. This could take from 30 to 45 minutes.

CLOSURE: Ask students, "What was important about this activity? What did you find interesting?"

PLEASE . . . PLEASE DON'T . . .

MATERIALS: two pieces of chart paper, markers

GROUPING: whole class

DIRECTIONS:

(1) At the first class meeting, talk with students about the need to come to consensus (agreement) on how "we want to be treated in this classroom."

(2) Discuss the process of brainstorming; emphasize the importance of accepting all ideas, with no putdowns or judgments.

(3) Question students about why it is important not to judge or put down others' ideas.

(4) Set up two charts, one labeled "Please . . ." and the other "Please Don't . . ."

(5) Ask students to generate endings to these two requests (think about whether you want them to yell out or raise their hands beforehand, and explain your chosen procedure before beginning).

(6) Discuss the students' comments as appropriate.

(7) Reread the charts at the end of the activity.

CLOSURE: Ask, "Why was it important to talk about this together? What can you do to help your classmates feel safe and comfortable here?"

——*Day 2: Please . . . Please Don't . . .*

DIRECTIONS:

(1) From looking at the lists made up the first day, come up with four to six rules that would incorporate all of the students' concerns. These rules should be (a) stated in positive terms, (b) broad enough to cover all general behaviors, and (c) stated simply.

(2) Transfer the lists that were generated the day before to the board. Explain to the class that you looked at their lists and could see some rules that seemed to cover all of their requests.

(3) Write the rules on the board with a lot of space between them. Tell the students that you want to be sure all of their concerns are covered, so you are going to go through their lists together and decide which rule each item would go under.

(4) Read the requests on the lists one by one and have the students tell you which rule to put each under. Allow discussion and negotiation. Keep going until all the requests have been covered.

(5) Discuss what to do when someone does something on the "Please Don't" list. Have students brainstorm a list of consequences and grade them from mild to severe. Use these rules as guidelines for the class.

ART ACTIVITIES

BRAINSTORMING: CHEERIOS

MATERIALS: one box of Cheerios, felt pens, crayons, one piece of butcher paper per group (20 × 30 inches)

GROUPING: cooperative groups of four

APPROXIMATE TIME: 90 minutes

DIRECTIONS:

(1) Tell the class that this is an activity that will exercise their creative thinking.

(2) Divide the class into groups of four and then have each group number off, 1 through 4. Assign each number a job: recorder, reporter, timekeeper, and gopher. (Write these on the board for reference.)

(3) Talk about what brainstorming is—accepting all ideas, no judgments. Then tell students they will be working on a creative art activity with Cheerios. First they will brainstorm uses for Cheerios, and then they will do an art project substituting Cheerios for objects in the picture.

(4) Have the student groups brainstorm lists of possible uses for Cheerios in a picture (rings, necklaces, wheels for cars, and so on). The group gophers get paper, and the recorders write their groups' ideas. The timekeepers allow 5 minutes for the task.

(5) Have the reporters come up front to share five of their groups' ideas. Record these ideas on the board for later use in the art project.

(6) Now have the groups work on an art project cooperatively. They will need to decide on a scene and what each person will be responsible for drawing. You may give each one a different color pen to be sure they all contribute. Each group will draw a scene, using Cheerios in place of drawn items as much as possible. For example, a car might have Cheerios as tires. Give approximately 45 minutes for the art project. Gophers distribute Cheerios and butcher paper.

(7) Have the groups share and talk about their projects with the class.

CLOSURE: Ask the groups how they decided on their scenes. Ask each group what made its project successful. Ask students within the groups to compliment each other for some specific contributions they made to the project.

EXTENSION: Have the student groups brainstorm analogies (write the words and definitions on the board): "A Cheerio is like a ___ because ___." Talk about the attributes of a Cheerio (shape, size, color, other qualities), and then brainstorm a few analogies as a class. Example: "A Cheerio is like a tire because it's round and has a hole in the middle." Have the recorders report their groups' analogies. Record these on the board.

ME PICTURES

MATERIALS: tagboard, construction paper, fabric scraps, yarn

GROUPING: whole class, individuals

APPROXIMATE TIME: two 60-minute periods

DIRECTIONS:

(1) Have students create pictures of themselves cut out of construction paper or tagboard, clothing themselves with fabric glued onto backing. When they draw their pictures, tell them to have their heads touch the top of the tagboard and their feet touch the bottom, so that the final pictures don't end up too small. (You should prepare a sample picture of yourself to show to students as an example.) Also, give them the tip that if the arms are too skinny, they'll look funny when they are cut out.

(2) Have students add cartoon bubbles to their pictures, showing them saying things they want to tell about themselves.

CLOSURE: Have each student share something he or she likes about his or her neighbor's picture.

EXTENSION: Have students create poems by writing adjectives that begin with each of the letters of their names to put up near their "me" pictures.

PARTNER DRAWINGS

MATERIALS: colored construction paper, various colors of pastel chalks (two per student)

GROUPING: whole class

APPROXIMATE TIME: 30-45 minutes

DIRECTIONS:

(1) Have music on quietly, in the background.
(2) Have students work in partner teams. Make sure each partner has two pieces of chalk, and that each partnership has one piece of paper. Tell students they may not talk during the art session.
(3) One partner starts by drawing any continuous line and stops. The next partner puts his or her chalk on the paper where the last line ended and draws any continuous line and stops. The work goes back and forth until, through nonverbal communication, the partners decide they are finished.

CLOSURE: Ask students, "What did you enjoy about the process? How did you and your partner decide when you were finished? How did you feel about your drawings?"

VARIATION: Both partners hold one piece of chalk together and create together, still with no talking. For closure on this activity, ask students, "Who was the leader? Did the leadership change? How did you feel?"

SHIELDS

MATERIALS: a shield for each student (make dittos of the black-line master [page 88] for practice shield and ditto onto 8 × 11-inch tagboard or construction paper for final copy), felt pens, crayons

GROUPING: individuals

APPROXIMATE TIME: 45-60 minutes

DIRECTIONS:

(1) Find some pictures of coats of arms or family shields in an encyclopedia. Show these to your students, and tell them that the pictures or emblems in the sections of these shields represent things about that family.

(2) Tell students that today they will be making their own shields. They will be getting a shield outline and will need to draw a picture and write a caption in each section. Today they will be making a practice copy and tomorrow they will make the final one.

(3) Draw a shield on the board and write a label in each section (see page 87). Students will fill in the shields with pictures or statements (or pictures with captions) for each label.

(4) Check for understanding, and then have paper monitors pass out the shield dittos. Circulate as the students begin, to be sure they understand what they should be doing.

CLOSURE: Tell the students you will look over their shields that night, help with editing, and return them tomorrow so they can make their final copies. Ask, "Why are family shields important? Did you realize something special about your family as you did this?"

——*Shields: Day 2*

DIRECTIONS: Return the practice shields and allow time for students to make their final shields on tagboard or white construction paper.

Know Your Classmate

create your own

SILHOUETTE MURALS

MATERIALS: large white butcher paper sheets covering wall space from floor to ceiling, pencils, projector, chalk, fixative spray, paper towels

GROUPING: partners or small groups; rest of class independent (could be practicing individual work with pastel chalks)

APPROXIMATE TIME: done over a period of a week; best started while the rest of the class works on individual art projects and as a finish-up time project

DIRECTIONS:

(1) Use one or more projectors to project silhouettes of students in various positions on the wall. Draw their outlines in pencil. (Be sure students stand sideways and that their eyelashes show up in their profiles, so they will know where the eyes are.)

(2) Start at the top of the paper, with students standing on desks or chairs, and work down the paper to having students kneel or sit. The silhouettes should overlap one another.

(3) Help students to draw in hairlines, neck lines, and cheek lines, and then have students color in their own figures with pastel chalks.

(4) You can teach the outlining technique to a small team who can help the rest of the students, or an adult can have the responsibility of helping each pair find its spot and get set up to draw. The coloring-in should be a sponge activity for students to work on when they finish other work.

TIPS:

(1) Have students practice using pastels by coloring in silhouettes on paper at their desks. Demonstrate how they can shade and mix colors with finger-rubbing motions.

(2) Have students use paper towels to keep their nondrawing hands from smudging the mural.

(3) Have students at the top of the mural color their faces first.

(4) Color in all faces before working on hair and clothes, so that no faces get covered.

(5) Spray a pastel fixative over the entire mural (do this after school, with all the windows open).

LITERACY ACTIVITIES (WITH SPANISH TRANSLATIONS)

FIND SOMEONE WHO . . .

MATERIALS: enough worksheets for all students, pencils

GROUPING: independent, whole class

APPROXIMATE TIME: 40 minutes

DIRECTIONS:

(1) Have students put their names on the tops of their worksheets, and then go over the "Someone Who" statements orally, so everyone can read them.

(2) Have students get as many people as possible to sign their names by the statements that apply to them. Students must ask, "Do you . . . ?" or "Have you ever . . . ?" before someone can sign their papers. (This is an activity to build language skills as well as get to know one another.)

(3) Tell students, "You may sign someone else's paper only once, and others can sign your paper only once each." Review the signal to stop.

(4) Call time when a few students are close to finishing their pages.

CLOSURE: Discuss who signed for each of the statements. You might want to graph the results. Ask students what they learned about their classmates.

Find someone who . . .

has three brothers._____

likes tortillas._____

plays baseball._____

likes to dance._____

was born in another country._____

likes rock music._____

has read *Ramona the Pest.*_____

eats cereal for breakfast._____

walks to school._____

can speak a language other than English._____

has a cat for a pet._____

has ridden a horse._____

has a truck in the family._____

has a baby in the family._____

has long hair._____

has a fireplace in his or her house._____

Encuentra a una persona que . . .

tiene tres hermanos._____

le gustan las tortillas._____

juega baseball._____

le gusta bailar._____

nació en otro país._____

le gusta la música rock._____

ha leído *Ramona la Chinche.*_____

come cereal en el desayuno._____

camina a la escuela._____

puede hablar otro idioma además de Inglés._____

tiene un gato mascota._____

ha montado un caballo._____

tiene un camión en su familia._____

tiene un bebé en su familia._____

tiene el cabello largo._____

tiene una chiminea en su casa._____

GRAFFITI BOARDS

MATERIALS: butcher paper cut into 15 × 36-inch pieces, glue, staplers, felt pens

GROUPING: individual

APPROXIMATE TIME: 45 minutes

DIRECTIONS:

(1) As homework the night before, ask students to bring in "three things from home that represent you and are important to you" to hang on a chart. Give examples: pictures, special clothing, awards, book jackets, and so on.

(2) Pass out the pieces of butcher paper and have the students write their names in large letters across the top and then glue or staple their items onto the paper. Explain what graffiti boards are and that graffiti can be an art form, but if written on buildings it can be a form of vandalism. Have a discussion about this.

(3) Display the graffiti boards on the bulletin board. Encourage students to write specific positive comments (model these, as well as nonspecific or inappropriate comments) on each others' graffiti boards during free time or independent work time.

(4) Discuss how someone might feel if his or her board had no comments. Ask the group to come up with a system to ensure this does not happen.

CLOSURE: Ask, "How did this activity make you feel? How might it be useful to our class as a whole? To individuals?"

LETTERS

MATERIALS: writing paper, pencils, enough teacher-written letters for all students, an envelope for each letter

GROUPING: whole class, individual

APPROXIMATE TIME: 20-30 minutes

DIRECTIONS:

(1) Before this class session, write a letter, leaving the name of the addressee blank. Make it friendly and chatty. In the letter, tell about yourself, what you like, your hobbies, and so on. You could include major units you have planned and ask for students' thoughts about school. At the end of the letter, ask them to write back to you, telling about themselves. Make enough copies for all your students. Before delivering the letters, address them individually with the students' names and put them in envelopes, also addressed individually.

(2) Pass out the letters. Generally, students' curiosity is piqued by this, and they begin without a lot of direction. If they don't begin working silently after 2-3 minutes, remind them of the procedures for independent work. Tell them they will have about 20 minutes to write their letters (this will vary with the grade level of the class). Tell them what they may do if they finish early (read a book, do a special worksheet you have ready, or whatever). Circulate to keep students on task and to encourage those who have a hard time starting.

(3) When you see everyone has finished, collect the letters and express your interest in reading them. (Save the letters to use in your student assessments; see Chapter 6.)

QUOTE DISCUSSION

MATERIALS: a meaningful quote, paper, pencils

GROUPING: variable (groups of four, individual, or whole class)

DIRECTIONS:

(1) Write a meaningful quote on the board.
(2) Ask students in cooperative groups to discuss what the quote means.
(3) Ask individuals to write down the quote, tell what it means, and give personal examples of how the quote applies to their own lives.
(4) Form a large circle and discuss what the quote means (no judgments) to different people.

CLOSURE: Ask the class, "What did you learn from this discussion?"

EXTENSIONS: This can be used as a homework assignment. Ask students to discuss the quote at home, at the dinner table, and report back.

——Famous Quotations

"Whether you think you can or think you can't—you are right."
HENRY FORD

"If it is to be . . . It is up to me."
WILLIAM JOHNSON

"Everyone has a fair turn to be as great as he pleases."
JEREMY COLLIER

"No one can make you feel inferior without your permission."
ELEANOR ROOSEVELT

"It's not so much what you do that makes you special. . . .
It's who you are."
ANONYMOUS

"Every job is a self-portrait of the person who did it. Autograph
your work with excellence."
ANONYMOUS

"The secret to success in any human endeavor is concentration."
KURT VONNEGUT

"Nothing great was ever achieved without enthusiasm."
RALPH WALDO EMERSON

"If you're not part of the solution, you're part of the problem."
M. SCOTT PECK

──*Dichos Famosos*
"Si crees que puedes o si crees que no puedes—tienes razón."
HENRY FORD

"Si algo ha de ser . . . ha de ser de mi voluntad."
WILLIAM JOHNSON

"No es tanto lo que haces que te valora, si no quien eres."
ANÓNIMO

"El secreto del éxito en cualquier empeño humano es la
concentración."
KURT VONNEGUT

"Sin entusiasmo, ninguno de los grandes hechos se hubieran
llevado a cabo."
RALPH WALDO EMERSON

"Si tu no eres parte de la solución, eres parte del problema."
M. SCOTT PECK

"El respeto al derecho ajeno, es la paz."
BENITO JUAREZ

WIGGLY LINE DRAWING

MATERIALS: enough worksheets for all students, pencils or crayons

GROUPING: independent

APPROXIMATE TIME: 45 minutes

DIRECTIONS:

(1) Place Wiggly Line worksheets and pencils or crayons on desks so that when students come in they can do this transition activity.

(2) Tell students to look at the worksheet and follow the instructions. As they are working, roam around the class to answer any questions and provide encouragement. Note anyone having trouble reading the directions or getting started writing.

(3) As students finish their work, be ready to put all of the worksheets directly up on the wall as a display of their drawing and writing.

(4) Look at the writing samples to note where each student is developmentally in his or her writing skills. Save this sample to use in one of your initial assessments.

CLOSURE: Read a few of the Wiggly Line stories to the class each day until they have all been shared. Ask the class to share some things they liked.

Wiggly Line / Línea Ondulada

Use this line to begin a picture. Then write a story about your picture.
Usa esta línea para comenzar un dibujo. Escribe un cuento sobre su dibujo.

_____

_____

_____

_____

_____

_____

_____

_____

Keys to the Classroom. © 1992 Corwin Press, Inc.

SELF-ASSESSMENTS (WITH SPANISH TRANSLATIONS)

STUDENT SELF-ASSESSMENT

MATERIALS: enough teacher-made worksheets for all students, pencils

GROUPING: whole class

APPROXIMATE TIME: 20-30 minutes

DIRECTIONS:

(1) Make your own worksheet or use one of the following examples of a self-assessment.

(2) Pass out the worksheets and explain this activity to the students. For example, you might say something such as: "The more we know about ourselves, the better choices we can make. This activity will help you reflect on or think about how you feel about things. I will collect and read these worksheets, but the information will remain private. The more thought you put into your answers, the more helpful this activity will be. You will have approximately 15 minutes to complete the worksheet. I will collect the papers when everyone is finished. If you finish early, you may silently read a book."

(3) Give the signal to begin, and then circulate around the room, keeping the students on task. You may want to fill out one of the worksheets yourself.

(4) When everyone has finished, give the zero-noise signal and collect the papers.

CLOSURE: Ask such questions as "Did anyone find a question difficult to answer? Which one? Why do you think it was difficult?" (Be prepared to volunteer your own responses. You are modeling for the students that the classroom is a safe place to share ideas and feelings.) Also, be sure to say, "Thank you for your honest responses. They will help me know you better."

Read the worksheets carefully. The responses will give you insight into your students' behavior and how they learn. Some students will be able to analyze their feelings better than others. Keep the worksheets in individual student folders. Do this activity periodically throughout the school year or just once more at the end of the year, and let the students compare their responses.

Student Self-Assessment

Write a sentence about each of the following statements.

(1) I like school.

_____

(2) I'm a responsible person.

_____

(3) I have many friends.

_____

(4) I have a close friend.

_____

(5) I like to read.

_____

(6) I'm comfortable reading aloud.

_____

(7) I write stories at home.

_____

(8) I'm a good writer.

_____

(9) I'm good at art.

_____

(10) I'm a leader.

_____

(11) I'm dependable.

_____

(12) I like science.

_____

(13) I'm cooperative.

_____

(14) I'm good at sports.

_____

(15) I'm a fair person.

_____

Keys to the Classroom. © *1992 Corwin Press, Inc.*

(16) My favorite subject is_____

(17) My least favorite subject is _____

(18) I'm good at_____

(19) I could improve in_____

(20) I read ___ hours a week.

If you would like to add or explain something, please use the back of the paper.

Evaluación Personal del Estudiante

Escriba un oración por cada uno de los siguientes.

(1) A mí me gusta la escuela.

_____

(2) Yo soy una persona responsable.

_____

(3) Yo tengo muchos amigos.

_____

(4) Yo tengo un amigo favorito.

_____

(5) A mí me gusta leer.

_____

(6) A mí no me molesta leer en voz alta.

_____

(7) Yo escribo cuentos en mi casa.

_____

Keys to the Classroom. © 1992 Corwin Press, Inc.

(8) Yo soy un buen escritor.

_____

(9) A mí me gustan las cosas artísticas.

_____

(10) Yo soy un líder.

_____

(11) Yo soy cumplidor.

_____

(12) A mí me gustan las ciencias.

_____

(13) A mí me gusta cooperar.

_____

(14) Yo soy un buen deportista.

_____

(15) Yo soy una persona justa.

_____

(16) Mi materia favorita es _____

(17) La materia que menos me gusta es_____

(18) Yo soy bueno en_____

(19) Yo podría mejorar en_____

(20) Yo leo __ horas a la semana.

Si quieres explicar o decir algo más, usa el otro lado de la hoja.

How I Feel

These sentences are not finished. Complete each sentence by writing what you feel. Remember, there are no right or wrong answers.

(1) I'm really interested in

(2) What I like best about myself is

(3) Sometimes I worry about

(4) I am happy when

(5) I get upset when

(6) If I could change myself, I would

(7) My best experience in school was

(8) I need help with

(9) I wish that

Como Siento Yo

Estas oraciones no están completas. Termina cada oración describiendo cómo te sientes. Recuerda, no hay contestaciones correctas o equivocadas.

(1) Lo que más me interesa es

(2) Lo que más me gusta acerca de mi mismo

(3) A veces lo que más me preocupa es

(4) Estoy feliz cuando

(5) Me da coraje cuando

(6) Si pudiera cambiar algo de mi mismo, cambiaría

(7) Mi mejor experiencia escolar fue

(8) Necesito ayuda con

(9) Yo quisiera que

What I Think About Reading

(1) How do I feel about reading?

(2) How much time do I read and when do I do it?

(3) When I can read anything I choose, I read (choose from these or add your own: newspapers, magazines, books, poems stories, letters, comics, directions to make things, etc.)

(4) I like to read books and stories about (choose from these or add your own: adventure, animals, girls, make-believe, history, boys, famous people, mystery, etc.)

(5) The best books or stories I have ever read were

(6) The things I don't like about reading are

(7) What I would like to do in reading this year is

(8) The way I will become a better reader is to

Lo Que Yo Opino de la Lectura

(1) ¿Cómo me siento acerca de la lectura?

(2) ¿Cuánto tiempo me paso leyendo y cuando leo?

(3) Cuando puedo leer cualquier cosa, yo escojo (escoge de éstos o añade otros tuyos: periódicos, revistas, libros, poemas, historias, cartas, direcciones para hacer cosas)

(4) Me gusta leer libros y cuentos acerca de (escoge de éstos o añade otros túyos: aventuras, animales, muchachas, cosas imaginarias, historia, muchachos, personas famosas, misterios)

(5) Los mejores libros o historias que yo he leído

(6) Lo que no me gusta acerca de la lectura es

(7) Lo que yo quisiera hacer este año en la clase de lectura es

(8) De la manera que voy a ser un mejor lector va a ser

What I Think About Writing

(1) How do I feel about writing?

(2) Choosing from this list, the kinds of writing I enjoy most are (letters, stories, poems, reports, plays, songs, or newspaper stories)

(3) The hardest thing about writing is

(4) The best things I've ever written were

(5) The reason they were so good (refer to number 4) was that

These are some things that make stories good: (a) a good beginning, (b) interesting characters, (c) good description, (d) action, (e) adventure, (f) suspense, (g) surprises, and (h) good endings.

(6) From the list above, some of the things I do well in my stories are

(7) Some of the things I would like to do better in my writing are

Lo Que Pienso Acerca de la Escritura

(1) ¿Cómo me siento acerca de la escritura?

(2) De la siguiente lista, el tópico para escribir que me daría más placer sería (cartas, cuentos, poemas, reportes, dramas, canciones, historias periódisticas)

(3) Lo más difícil para poder escribir es

(4) Las mejores cosas que he escrito son

(5) La razón por la cual son tan buenas (refiere al numero 4) es

Estas son algunas de las cosas que un buen cuento contiene: (a) un buen principio, (b) personajes interesantes, (c) buena descripción, (d) acción, (e) aventuras, (f) suspenso, (g) sorpresas, y (h) un buen final.

(6) De la lista anterior algunas de las cosas que yo hago bien en mis cuentos son

(7) Algunas de las cosas que quisiera hacer mejor cuando escribo son

Keys to the Classroom. © 1992 Corwin Press, Inc.

MATH ACTIVITIES

MATH CHALLENGES

MATERIALS: math journals, pencils

GROUPING: individual

APPROXIMATE TIME: 15-20 minutes

DIRECTIONS:

(1) Begin the math period with a brief challenge activity. Have a place on the board where the math challenge is written each day, so students can get started when they come in. The challenge might be from any of the math strands, or might focus on the computational process you are currently teaching. You might want to make up math problems using information that is relevant to your class or that fits in with what you are studying in other content areas (e.g., if you're studying marine life, your problems could be about otters, fish, and so on).

(2) Have students work the math challenge problem in their math journals (see the math journal activity below).

(3) When the time is up, discuss the various strategies students used to solve the problem. Have several students come to the board to share their diagrams and equations and tell about the various strategies they used to solve the problem. Encourage the students to draw pictures to show their solutions and have them write equations to explain their computations.

——*Examples of Challenges*

(1) How much will a dozen six-cent stamps cost? ($12 \times \$.06 = \$ .72$)

(2) There are 11 clothespins strung on a line. Each clothespin is six centimeters from the previous clothespin. How many centimeters is it from the first clothespin to the last clothespin? ($6 \times 10 = 60$ cm)

(3) If eggs cost 96 cents a dozen, how many eggs can you by for three quarters, two dimes, and one penny? ($\$.75 + \$.20 + \$.01 = \$.96$; one dozen)

(4) One place charges $39.00 a day to rent a car. Another place charges $58.00 a day. How much can you save by renting the car from the first place rather than the second? ($\$58.00 - \$39.00 = \$19.00$)

(5) Mom has four pies. She wants to cut them so each of eight people has the same size piece. What is the size of each piece? ($4 + 8 = \frac{1}{2}$ pie for each piece)

(6) Ron had _____ rose bushes. She went to the garden shop and bought 9 more. How many plants did she buy if she has 21 in all? (21 − 9 = 12)

(7) Estimate how many shoelace holes are in our class today.

(8) Apples cost 43 cents a pound. How many pounds of apples did I buy if I spent $2.15? ($2.15 ÷ 43 = 5 lbs.)

En Español

(1) ¿Cuánto cuesta una docena de timbres de seis centavos? (12 × $.06 = $.72)

(2) Once ganchos están en la linea. Cada gancho está a seis centimetros de cada uno. ¿Cuántos centímetros hay del primer gancho al último? (6 × 10 = 60 cm)

(3) ¿Si una docena de blanquillos cuesta 96 centavos, cuántos blanquillos puedes comprar con tres "quarters," dos "dimes," y un centavo? ($.75 + $.20 + $.01 = $.96; una docena)

(4) En un lugar cobran $39.00 al día por rentar un carro. Otro lugar cobra $58.00 al día. ¿Cuánto puedes ahorrar si rentas el carro en el primer lugar en lugar del segundo lugar? ($58.00 − $39.00 = $19.00)

(5) Una madre tiene cuatro pasteles. Ella quiere cortar ocho pedazos para que cada persona ténga pedazos del mismo tamaño. ¿Cuál es el tamaño de cada pedazo? ($\frac{1}{2}$ pastel para cada uno)

(6) Rosa tenía _____ rosales. Ella fué a la jardinería y compró 9 más. ¿Cuántos rosales compró si tenía 21 en total? (21 − 9 = 12 rosales)

(7) ¿Aproximadamente, cuántos hojillos hay en todos los zapatos en la clase?

(8) Las manzanas cuestan 43 centavos la libra. ¿Cuántas libras de manzanas compré hoy si gasté $2.15? ($2.15 ÷ 43 = 5 lbs.)

THE CLASS AGE

MATERIALS: calculators (if possible, one for every two students)

GROUPING: partners

APPROXIMATE TIME: 30-40 minutes

DIRECTIONS:

(1) Have each student guess what the sum of everyone's age will be. Record the estimates on the board.

(2) Give each set of partners a calculator. If this is their first time with calculators, give students some time to play around with them; let them know what is acceptable and what is not. Go over the functions of the keys, and do a couple of practice problems. Also go over the care and handling of a calculator.

(3) Review teacher-led lesson procedures.

(4) Go around the class, asking each student how old he or she is. Have the partners enter each age in their calculators and then push the + key. Ask for a subtotal after each entry. If any pair has made an error, they can clear the calculator and start again with the correct subtotal.

(5) Compare the results with the estimates.

EXTENSIONS:

(1) Graph the above activity.

(2) Do the above activity with other attributes, such as the combined heights of class members. How long a line would the class make if all the students lay down head to toe? Older students could also find the average, range, and median age, height, or whatever.

COOPERATIVE TRIANGLES

MATERIALS: enough copies of the cooperative triangle (see next page) for all students, crayons, pencils, felt pens

GROUPING: cooperative groups of three

APPROXIMATE TIME: 30 minutes

DIRECTIONS:

(1) Have students work in groups of three to count all the triangles in the figure. Assign group jobs: recorder, reporter, and facilitator (checks for agreement, keeps discussion going, makes sure everyone participates).

(2) Each group must come up with a strategy for keeping track of the triangles counted.

(3) Give approximately 5 minutes for the task.

(4) Have the reporters share their groups' findings. Have facilitators tell about the strategies their groups used in keeping track of the triangles.

CLOSURE: Come to consensus, if possible. There is no need to tell the answer; some students will pursue the problem.

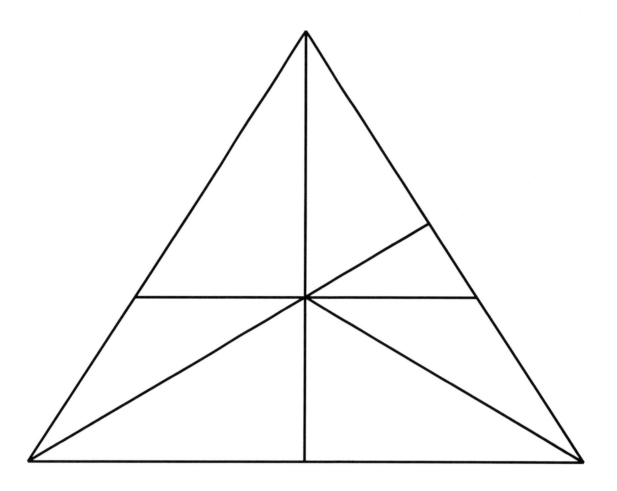

PROBLEM-SOLVING STRATEGIES: ESTIMATING RAISINS

MATERIALS: construction paper, scrap paper, crayons, felt pens, one ½-ounce box of raisins for each cooperative group

GROUPING: cooperative groups of four

APPROXIMATE TIME: 30 minutes

DIRECTIONS:

(1) Write the following directions on the board:
   (a) As a group, estimate how many raisins are in a ½-ounce box.
   (b) Write the estimate and tell how you came up with it. Recorder writes group's ideas.
   (c) Open the box and count how many raisins are in it. Determine a strategy for counting them quickly.
   (d) Write the number of actual raisins in your box and tell the difference between the estimated and actual number of raisins.
   (e) Divide the raisins equally among the members of your group.
   (f) Draw a picture of each member's share of raisins.
   (g) Write an equation or number sentence for dividing the raisins.
(2) Explain to the students that they will be working in cooperative groups. Each person will have a role: The gopher will distribute and collect the materials; the recorder will write down what group members say; the leader will make sure everyone participates equally, using positive praise; and the timekeeper will keep the group on task and on time. Assign roles to students by having them number off and making all number ones gophers, and so on.
(3) Read over the directions written on the board, modeling an example of how the task might be done and reviewing what each of the roles might look like during the process. Review cooperative group procedures with the class.
(4) Explain that when the groups finish they will all have group sheets that explain the process of how they solved the problem. These group sheets will all be put into a class book.

CLOSURE: When their group sheet has been turned in, have the group discuss and write how they divided up the task and what made the group work well.

EVALUATION: Gather on the rug and discuss what criteria should be evaluated: neatness/organization, content, correctness, enhancements. Go through all of the group sheets and evaluate them together against the chosen criteria (you might assign 10 points to each area). In this way you will model evaluation for the class for future journal entries. You may graph your results.

MATH JOURNAL

MATERIALS: folders for all students with graph or grid paper stapled inside, pencils

GROUPING: whole class, individual

APPROXIMATE TIME: variable

DIRECTIONS:

(1) Explain to your students that math journals are places where they write about how to solve math problems. They will provide students with an opportunity to think through their strategies for solving problems, so that they may apply those strategies in other situations. (These journals also provide you with valuable information on students' problem-solving skills. They are also a great way to integrate math and writing skills and to develop expository writing skills.)

(2) Use the raisin estimation activity to have students begin the process of math journals in a cooperative setting. After the activity, explain that the students' journals will be evaluated in the same way the class book was.

(3) Give each student a folder with graph or grid paper stapled inside to use as a math journal. Have the students begin their journals by reflecting on the process of doing math cooperatively in the raisin estimation activity. Ask, "What do you like about doing math cooperatively, compared with doing it alone?" Discuss/share some entries from volunteers.

(4) Use journals a few times a month as an in-depth project. Have students explain/illustrate the process of solving a problem.

(5) Use journals daily to work on/record math challenge problems.

(6) Have students use the journals also to record their feelings about math and to create their own math problem stories. Have students reflect on their experience in math and what they have learned or what they are having difficulty with.

ASSESSMENT: Collect six to eight journals each week to assess (everyone is assessed monthly). Skim through and make some notes in your anecdotal record log about students' thinking skills (logical, sequential, organizational strategies). Use the criteria the class decided on for evaluation (neatness, content, correctness, enhancements). You may want to photocopy a page or two of each student's journal to keep in his or her math folder, to show thinking skills to parents or to show strengths or weaknesses in strategies.

GRAPHING

MATERIALS: paper, pencils, pens, graph paper, chart paper

GROUPING: partners

APPROXIMATE TIME: 45 minutes

DIRECTIONS:

(1) Have the students work in pairs. Pair them up ahead of time, have them count off, or let them self-select their partners.

(2) Discuss the types of questions the class used in Partner Introductions to get to know their classmates. Record the questions on the board.

(3) Have each pair of students select a question, or assign a question to each pair.

(4) Let the pairs work together to decide the type of graph they want to make and how they should record the information. Review various types of graphs and have samples of each available. For younger students, decide the type of graph they should use and teach them how to collect the data.

(5) Give the class 10 minutes to move around the room to get the data for their graphs.

(6) Have students return to their seats to begin work on their graphs. Supply pens, graph paper, and chart paper. While the students are working, encourage them to work together and to do their best work on the graphs. Mention some elements of a useful graph: a title, clearly labeled information, legibility, and so on.

(7) When the graphs are complete, have each pair write a sentence explaining what their graph says. Display the graphs in the room as a student-made bulletin board.

EXTENSION: Have students create surveys to take home and use to survey five people. Have them create graphs using the new information with their partners the next day.

PEOPLE MEASURING

MATERIALS: enough pieces of string for all students to have several (cut each piece longer than the tallest student in the class), masking tape, pencils

GROUPING: partners

APPROXIMATE TIME: 30-40 minutes

DIRECTIONS:

(1) Go over the procedures for a teacher-led lesson with small groups.

(2) Have students pair up. You can assign partners ahead of time or have the students number off. The important part is that no one feels left out and that everyone has a partner.

(3) Pass out several pieces of string to each student. (Older students could do this activity using meter sticks or tape measures.)

(4) First, have the students, in pairs, help each other measure and cut their pieces of string to the exact height of their partners. Then have them measure each others' arm spans, and cut a string to that length. Give the students time to complete the measuring (and recording, for older students) while you circulate. Give them masking tape to label which body part each piece of string represents; have them initial their labels. The students may continue measuring arms, legs, head circumference, and so on in the same way.

(5) Have the students graph their findings in one or more of the following ways. Tape all the strings representing height, arm span, and so on along a wall on one piece of masking tape to see all the different lengths, creating a string graph. Have students measure their strings with rulers, convert their measurements from feet and inches to meters and centimeters, and graph the class.

(6) Have students look at relationships between height and arm span or height and head circumference, and so on, making predictions and testing them out. Record the results and compare what they find. Have them tell how their measurements compare; for example, "My height is three times the circumference of my head."

HOMEWORK IDEAS

Homework should reinforce in-class work or prepare students for a coming lesson whenever possible. Part of the purpose of homework is to teach study habits at home. It is important to discuss with students how they might set up a routine to get homework done and put in a special place, so they will remember to bring it back. There should be a basket near the classroom door for turning in homework. It can be checked in quickly by an instructional aide or a student. Assigning numbers to be placed in the upper left-hand corners of papers that correspond with a class record list will facilitate putting papers in order to check off. Send a letter home to parents to inform them of the homework schedule. (See Chapter 7 for a sample.)

Ideas for Homework Assignments

- Read silently or to a brother, sister, or parent for 30 minutes (this can be signed off in a notebook by a parent).
- Write a story based on a story starter such as "The worst day of my life . . . " or "The best party I can imagine . . . ."
- Study math facts related to current in-class math work.
- Walk through your house/neighborhood looking for all the things whose names start with a certain letter, particular sounds, particular smells, things using electricity, things that are living, things that come from different countries, and so on.
- Interview family members on different issues.
- Look for all the pictures, television shows, foods, fabrics, colors, and so on that relate to a particular thematic unit coming up in class.
- Survey neighbors, friends, and family to graph the next day.
- Write about or draw who lives in your house, including at least two adjectives about each person.
- Draw the name of a classmate from a hat in class, and write a description of that person to use in a "guess who" game.
- Write a letter to a relative, a political leader, or a company to bring in for editing and revision.

SPONGE ACTIVITIES

Sponge activities are so named because they soak up time. They should be fun activities that can be done spontaneously, enhancing learning in subtle ways. Ask your class to brainstorm their favorite games from previous years and keep a list. Have students model the games for the rest of the class when you are ready to play. Some ideas they will probably come up with are Around the World, Multiplication Baseball, and Heads-Up 7-Up.

Keys to the Classroom. © 1992 Corwin Press, Inc.

Old Reliable Sponges

➤ *People Sorting:* Think of a rule in your mind, such as students with short sleeves. Call students to come and stand next to you in front of the class. Those that follow the rule (who are wearing short sleeves) stand on your right; others stand on your left. Ask the class if they can guess your rule. Any students who think they know the rule must tell you which side they should stand on. Keep sorting students until you think many people know the rule, then ask them to say what they think your rule is. This is very good for vocabulary development (for learning such words as denim, velcro, collars, pullovers, jewelry, beige).

➤ *Line-Ups:* Have the whole class line up around the room in some of the following ways: in order of birth dates, alphabetical order by first or last name, distance they live from the school, furthest point they've ever traveled to, shortest to tallest. Variation: Pass out pictures to use for fastest to slowest transportation, biggest to smallest animal, and so on. Ask students to share what they learned during this activity. Ask what other ways they might line up.

➤ *Mastermind:* Students try to guess a word you're thinking of by guessing letters. They get an X for each right letter in the right place. They get an O for a right letter but in the wrong place, and they get a dash for a wrong letter. They try to use the fewest guesses possible.

➤ *20 Questions:* Have the students try to guess something you are thinking of by asking only yes or no questions. They have 20 questions. Teach the students some questioning strategies that start out in broad categories and narrow down, such as "Is it animal, vegetable, or mineral?" (This is a "free" question, and the only non-yes/no question allowed.) If an animal, "Is it a reptile?" If no, "Is it a mammal?" If yes, "Does it live on land?" If no, "Does it live in water?" And so on. One variation on this game is to have students guess a number rather than an object. Encourage them to use terms such as *greater than, less than, odd, even, a multiple of, in the 60s.* Another variation uses careers (What's My Line?). Instead of just yes or no questions, students can ask, "Would you . . . " questions, with possible answers being "every day," "sometimes," "hardly ever," and "never."

➤ *Wonderball:* While passing a ball around a circle, the class chants: "The wonderball goes round and round / to pass it quickly you are bound. / If you're the one to hold it last, / then for you the game has passed." The one holding the ball when the chant ends is out. Keep rounds short, so students can get back into the game.

➤ *Switch:* Two students go out of the room while everyone else changes seats. When the two come back in, they must return misplaced students to their correct desks within 3 minutes. (Remove student name cards from desks.)

➡ *Clap Action:* One student goes out of the room and the rest of the class decides on an action, such as washing hands or touching the chalkboard. The student returns and tries to guess the action by moving to different areas of the room and trying out different movements. The class guides him or her by clapping louder and louder as the student gets closer to the correct task. A variation on this game, You're Hot, has students call out "You're getting warmer" (moving toward it) or "You're getting colder" (moving away from it) as a student tries to find a hidden object.

➡ *Categories:* Sitting with the class in a circle, start a rhythm of clapping and hitting knees. Choose a category (for instance, presidents) and say, "Categories, presidents." Then, each person in turn around the circle has to name a president before two rhythm claps have gone by or they are out. There are many other categories you can use, such as fruits, domestic animals, words beginning with a certain letter, authors, television shows, and adjectives.

➡ *Safari:* Decide on a category of attributes (in this example, things with four legs) that will be the same about all the things you are taking on an imaginary safari; tell students they can come with you if they bring the correct kinds of items. You say, "I'm going on a safari and I'm taking an elephant and a chair." If a student wants to go on safari with you, he or she must say, "I'm going with you, and I'm bringing a table (or a dog, or a something else that has four legs)." Students who name the right kinds of items then get up and stand with you in front of the class. If a student wants to bring the wrong kind of item, you say, "Sorry, you can't come." You can vary this game by using other kinds of trips (picnics, vacations) and by using beginning letter sounds, two-syllable words, or other attributes of the words rather than the objects.

➡ *My Aunt Likes Coffee But She Doesn't Like Tea:* Write a couple of items on the board that follow a pattern. Students have to guess other things that fit into the pattern of something "your aunt" would like. For example, using beginning letter sounds, she might like cookies, cakes, coffee, and camping, but not pies, turnovers, tea, or backpacking. As with Safari, you can vary this game by using different patterns: word ending sounds, number of syllables, and so on.

➡ *Function Machine:* Draw a picture of or create a three-dimensional function machine that you can put numbers into and change them to something else. The functions can get more and more complex as students get better at the game. Example: "I put in 3 and out comes 9, I put in 6 and out comes 12. What is the function?" (Add 6.) "I put in a 3 and out comes 10, I put in a 4 and out comes 13, I put in a 5 and out comes 16. What is the function?" (Multiply by 3 and add 1.)

P.E. IDEAS

Think out your procedures for each game. Explain any new games prior to leaving the classroom, using drawings on the chalkboard if necessary. Explain to the class the proper dress for P.E.—tennis shoes and shorts or pants. Remind students of the attention signal to be used outside. Allow two minutes for students to change and meet the class outside. Set the procedures for choosing teams if necessary, and remind students about the "no putdown" rule. For team games, either you or team captains should choose equal teams at another time to be ready for P.E. Vary the types of activities so that not just the athletically inclined enjoy success at P.E. time.

Besides the games suggested below, relay races, four square, kickball, softball, soccer, and basketball are old standbys that your students will be wanting to learn.

- *Steal the Bacon:* Create two lines and have them both number off, so each student has a number; have the lines stand opposite each other, with some space in between. When you call out a number, those students who have that number run out, steal the "bacon" (chalkboard eraser) from the center, and run back over their lines. The one who makes it first gets a point.

- *Steal the Basket:* This is the same as Steal the Bacon, but the students steal a basketball, dribble, and try to make a basket.

- *Knots:* Divide the class into three groups. Each group forms a circle, shoulder to shoulder, and then each student grabs hands with anyone who is not standing next to him or her. Each student must hold the hands of two different people. When these "knots" are all tied, the groups try to untangle the mess without ever letting go of hands. Students must step over and under, twist and turn, but never drop a hand. If a group comes to a deadlock, the teacher may make one break to help them move on. (This and the next game are from *The New Games Book*, by Andrew Fluegelman.)

- *The Lap Game:* Form a circle with everyone facing in one direction. One person lies down, with knees bent and feet flat on the ground. The next person sits down on the first person's knees, forming an easy-chair "lap" for the next person to sit in. This proceeds around the circle until everyone is sitting on each others' laps. The hard part is hoisting up the person who formed the initial "lap" to sit on the person behind.

- *T-Ball:* This is a noncompetitive form of baseball, good for young beginners to practice their skills. Set the two teams up just as in baseball, but instead of getting outs each student gets a turn at bat and then you change sides. There is no pitcher; the ball is placed on a tee for the batter to swing at it. Don't keep track of runs—this game is just for fun and practice.

5 Fingerplays and Songs for Oral Language in English and Spanish

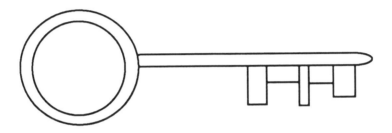

Fingerplays and songs are excellent for oral language development in primary grades. They are also very effective for second-language learning at any age. The interaction of visual cues, kinesthetic movements, and comprehensible language combined with rhythm makes them easily committed to memory. They can be used to build a base of common vocabulary in your class. They are also wonderful transition activities or sponges to bring students together and get them ready for the next activity.

CHAPTER CONTENTS

ATTENTION-GETTING FINGERPLAYS

These fingerplays are those you should start when you need the group's attention. Learn at least two or three to use the first week of school, then add one each week. You will find you use them all year.

Good Morning
(sung to the tune of "Are You Sleeping?")

Good morning, good morning.
How are you? How are you?
Very well, thank you.
Very well, thank you.
How are you? How are you?

Buenos Días

Buenos días, buenos días.
¿Cómo está? ¿Cómo está?
Muy bien, gracias.
Muy bien, gracias.
¿Y usted? ¿Y usted?

Open Them, Shut Them

Open them, shut them. [hands]
Open them, shut them.
Give your hands a clap.
Open them, shut them.
Open them, shut them.
Fold them in your lap.

Abranlas, Ciérrenlas

Abranlas, ciérrenlas.
Abranlas, ciérrenlas.
Pla, pla, pla.
Abranlas, ciérrenlas.
Abranlas, ciérrenlas.
Pónganlas acá.

One Little Eye

One little eye goes wink, wink, wink.
Two little eyes go blink, blink, blink.
One little hand goes snap, snap, snap.
Two little hands go clap, clap, clap.
Now fold them quietly in your lap.

Cinco Cochinitos

Cinco cochinitos vi por mi ventana.
Este trajo un huevo.
Este encendió el fuego.
Este trajo la sal.
Este lo guisó.
Y este pícaro gordo, se lo comió.

Head, Shoulders, Knees, and Toes

(This song may be done first in normal rhythm, then slow motion, then fast motion, to get lots of energy out.)

Head and shoulders, knees and toes,
Knees and toes.
Head and shoulders, knees and toes,
Knees and toes.
Eyes and ears and mouth and nose,
Head and shoulders, knees and toes,
Knees and toes.

De Cabeza a los Dedos

Cabeza, hombros, rodillas y dedos,
Rodillas y dedos.
Cabeza, hombros, rodillas y dedos,
Rodillas y dedos.
Ojos, orejas, boca, y nariz,
Cabeza, hombros, rodillas y dedos,
Rodillas y dedos.

Ten, Two, and One

I have 10 fingers, I have 10 toes.
I have 2 ears and 1 little nose.
I have 2 eyes, 1 mouth, 1 chin.
I have 1 tongue that moves out and in.

How Many Fingers?

Do you know? Do you know?
How many fingers I'm going to show?

(Show a number of fingers. Group counts and responds.)

Retintín

Retintín, retintón
¿Cúantos, cúantos dedos son?

Touch

Touch your shoulders,
Touch your knees,
Raise your arms,
Then drop them please.
Touch your ankles,
Then touch your toes,
Pull your ears,
Then touch your nose.
With your toes go
Tap, tap, tap.
Now your fingers
Snap, snap, snap.
Stretch as high as high can be.
While you're there,
Clap one, two, three.

Toca

Mis hombritos, mis rodillas,

Así extiendo mis brazitos,

Mis tobillos, y mis pies,

Mis oidos, enseño diez (dedos).

Con mis pies me paro así,

Y mis dedos trueno así.

Luego yo me estiro pues,

Y aplaudo uno, dos, tres.

Where Is Thumbkin?

Where is Thumbkin?

Where is Thumbkin?

Here I am.

Here I am.

How are you today, sir?

Very well I thank you.

Run away, run away.

Repeat, substituting for the first two lines:

Where is Pointer?

Where is Tall Finger?

Where is Ring Finger?

Where is Little Finger?

Where is everybody?

Mi Cuerpo y Yo

Yo me levanto, estoy de pie.

Cuento los dedos, uno, dos, tres.

Abro la boca, cierro los ojos.

Me toco los labios que son rosas.

Giro a la derecha, estoy contento,

Saco la lengua por un momento.

Abro los ojos, miro al cielo.

Me toco la cabeza, cubierto de pelo,

Doy palmadas, levanto el brazo.

Giro a la izquierda y doy un paso.

INCLUSION SONGS

These songs either use the children's own names or involve the group in making up new verses. In these ways, they help the children feel part of the class.

The More We Get Together

The more we get together, together, together,

The more we get together,

The happier you'll be.

There's [child's name] and [child's name] [continue to name children as they are ready, or you want to excuse them to line, or whatever]

The happier you'll be.

Lo Más Que nos Juntamos

Lo más que nos juntamos, juntamos, juntamos,

Lo más que nos juntamos,

Más contento/a estoy.

Hay [nombre de un niño] y [otro nombre] [diga los nombres de los niños que

estan listos, o para dejar a unos irse a la fila, o por cualquier razón]

Más contento/a estoy.

If You're Happy and You Know It

If you're happy and you know it, clap your hands.

If you're happy and you know it, clap your hands.

If you're happy and you know it,

Then your face will surely show it.

If you're happy and you know it, clap your hands.

If you're happy and you know it, tap your foot.

If you're happy and you know it, tap your foot.

If you're happy and you know it,

Then your face will surely show it.

If you're happy and you know it, tap your foot.
    (Ask the children to give other motions. Sing each.)

Si Felices Están Todos

Si felices están todos, aplauden.

Si felices están todos, aplauden.

Si felices están todos, si felices están todos,

Si felices están todos aplauden.
    (Pida a los niños otros movimientos y los canten en la canción.)

Cookie Jar

Group: Who stole the cookie from the cookie jar?

[Name of child] stole the cookie from the cookie jar.

Individual: Who me?

Group: Yes, you!

Individual: Couldn't be!

Group: Then who?

Individual: [Name of another child.]
   (Group begins the chant again with that child's name, and so on.)

Rhythm Chant

Start a snap, clap, slap knees rhythm. Have the children join with you. Then, on each snap, say a child's name. Go around the group, saying each child's name in turn. For example: clap, slap knees, José (snap while saying José); clap, slap knees, María; clap, slap knees, Wendy; and so on.

Ambos a Dos

This traditional circle game starts with one child in the center while the other children walk around him or her and sing. The child in the center names another child to join him or her. That child then names another and so on, until all are in the center.

Ambos a dos, matarile, rile.

Ambos a dos, matarile, rile, ron.

¿Quíen quiere usted?

Matarile, rile, rile.

¿Quíen quiere usted?

Matarile, rile, ron.

Quiero a [nombre de un niño].

Matarile, rile, rile.

Quiero a [nombre de un niño].

Matarile, rile, ron.
   (The first verse should be taught in Spanish. *Matarile, rile, rile* is roughly equivalent to tra-la-la. Then:)

Who will you choose?

Matarile, rile, rile.

Who will you choose?

Matarile, rile, rile.

I'll choose [name of child].

Matarile, rile, rile.

I'll choose [name of child].

Matarile, rile, rile.

Sally Go Round the Sun

As the group sings this song, one child skips around the outside of the circle (substitute that child's name for "Sally" after the children have learned the song). On the words "Every afternoon," he or she taps another child to trade places. Repeat.

Sally [or other child's name] go round the sun.

Sally go round the moon.

Sally go round the chimney pot

Every afternoon.

Johnny Works With One Hammer

Johnny [or any child's name] works with one hammer, one hammer, one hammer [pounding motion with one hand],

Johnny works with one hammer, then he works with two.

Johnny works with two hammers, two hammers, two hammers [pounding motion with both hands],

Johnny works with two hammers, then he works with three.

Johnny works with three hammers, three hammers, three hammers [add foot to pounding motions],

Johnny works with three hammers, then he works with four.

Johnny works with four hammers, four hammers, four hammers [jump up and down, still making pounding motions with hands],

Johnny works with four hammers, then he works with five.

Johnny works with five hammers, five hammers, five hammers [add head nodding to other motions]

Johnny works with five hammers, then he goes to sleep. [lay head on hands]

Juanito tiene un martillo, un martillo, un martillo.

Juanito tiene un martillo, y luego tiene dos.

. . . con dos, tres, cuatro, y cinco, y luego se va a dormir.

SONGS THAT ARE ADAPTABLE TO THEMATIC UNITS

Often it is difficult to find enough songs and poems specifically suited to a particular topic. The following songs/chants can be adapted to fit any thematic unit. Just make some simple stick puppets, and you have an instant dramatization.

Five Little Monkeys (Bears, Elephants, Pumpkins)

Five little monkeys jumping on the bed.

One fell off and bumped his head.

Mommy called the doctor

And the doctor said,

"No more monkeys jumping on the bed!"
     (Repeat, counting down verse by verse to one monkey.)

Cinco Changuitos (Osos, Elefantes, Calabazas)

Cinco changuitos brincando en la cama.

Uno se cayó y se rompió la cabeza.

Mamá llamó al doctor

Y el doctor le dijo:

"¡Qué no brinquen más los changuitos en la cama!"

One Elephant (Bear, Car, Dinosaur) Went Out to Play

One elephant went out to play

On a spider's web one day.

He had such enormous fun,

He called for another elephant to come.

Two elephants went out to play.

On a spider's web one day.

They had such enormous fun,

They called for another elephant to come.
   (Continue with three to ten elephants.)

Un Elefante (Oso, Carro, Dinosaurio) Se Balanceaba

Un elefante se balanceaba

Sobre la tela de una araña.

Como veía que resistía,

Fué a llamar a otro elefante.

Dos elefantes se balanceaban

Sobre la tela de una araña.

Como veía que resistían,

Fueron a llamar a otro elefante.
   (Sigue con tres hasta diez.)

Ten Little Brown Bears (Dinosaurs, Ants) (sung to the tune of "Ten Little Indians")

One little, two little, three little brown bears,

Four little, five little, six little brown bears,

Seven little, eight little, nine little brown bears,

Ten little brown bears in a row.

Diez Ositos (Dinosaurios, Hormigas)

Uno, dos, tres ositos,

Cuatro, cinco, seis ositos.

Siete, ocho, nueve ositos.

Diez ositos chiquitos.

The Little Turtle

There was a little turtle

Who lived in a box.

She swam in the puddles

And climbed on the rocks.

She snapped at a mosquito,

She snapped at a flea,

She snapped at a minnow,

And she snapped at me.

She caught the mosquito,

She caught the flea,

She caught the minnow,

But she didn't catch me.

La Tortuguita

Había una tortuguita

Que en una cajito vivía.

En un charco nadaba

Y a las rocas subía.

Le tiraba mordiscos a un mosquito,

Le tiraba mordiscos a una pulga,

Le tiraba mordiscos a un pececito,

Y le tiraba mordiscos a mí.

Agarró el mosquito,

Agarró la pulga,

Agarró el pececito,

Pero no me alcanzó a mí.

Follow-Up Activity

(1) Repeat the chant many times, until the children have it memorized. Once the poem has been well learned, use it as the basis for an innovation related to something you have been studying. Brainstorm another animal to be the turtle, then brainstorm what that animal might eat and where that animal might live.

(2) Rewrite "The Little Turtle" on sentence strips. Leave blanks for the name of the animal, where it lives, and what it eats. Make word cards from your brainstormed list. Fill in the blanks with the word cards to make a new poem. You can try many variations and combinations of words until the children feel they have a final version. An example of an innovation follows:

There was a little bear
Who lived in the woods.
She swam in the river
And climbed on the bank.
She snapped at a salmon,
She snapped at a bee,
She snapped at a blueberry,
And she snapped at me.

Songs/Poems for a Bear Theme

The songs and chants above can all be adapted to a bear theme; here are a few other songs you won't need to adapt.

The Three Bear Chant

(Start a clap, slap knees rhythm. Then begin the chant.)
Once upon a time in a nursery rhyme
There were three bears, cha, cha, cha.
One was the papa bear,
One was the mama bear,
And one was the wee bear, cha, cha, cha.
One day they went a-walking,
One day they went a-talking
In the deep dark woods.
Along came the girl with the long golden hair.
She knocked, but no one was there.
Then along came the three bears:
"Someone's been eating my porridge,"
Said the papa bear, said the papa bear. [say the second "said the papa bear" in a deep voice]
"Someone's been eating my porridge,"

Said the mama bear, said the mama bear. [use a mama bear voice]

"Hey bob-a-ree bear," said the little wee bear, [baby bear voice]

"Someone has made my bowl bare."

"Someone's been sitting in my chair,"

Said the papa bear, said the papa bear.

"Someone's been sitting in my chair,"

Said the mama bear, said the mama bear.

"Hey bob-a-ree bear," said the little wee bear,

"Someone has broken my chair."

"Someone's been sleeping in my bed,"

Said the papa bear, said the papa bear.

"Someone's been sleeping in my bed,"

Said the mama bear, said the mama bear.

"Hey bob-a-ree bear," said the little wee bear,

"Someone is sleeping right there."

Then Goldilocks woke up

And that party broke up and

She ran right out of there.

That is the story of the three bears,

Cha, cha, cha.

The Bear Went Over the Mountain

The bear went over the mountain,

The bear went over the mountain,

The bear went over the mountain,

To see what he could see.
        (Ask the children to tell you what the bear saw. Sing each response in the blanks.)

He saw _____,

He saw _____,

He saw _____,

That is what the bear saw.

El Oso Subió la Montaña

El oso subió la montaña

El oso subió la montaña

El oso subió la montaña

Para ver que pudo ver.

El vió un(a) _____,

El vió un(a) _____,

El vió un(a) _____,

Este es lo que vió.

Oso Cafe, Oso Cafe

This is a translation of *Brown Bear, Brown Bear*, by Bill Martin, to use as a chant. You can make copies of the animals from the book and place them on the bulletin board, and then use them to chant the book repeatedly during whole-group circle time.

Oso Cafe, oso cafe,

¿Quién te mira a tí?

Veo un pájaro rojo mirándome a mí.

Pájaro rojo, pájaro rojo,

¿Quién te mira a tí?

Veo un [etc.]

Songs/Poems for a Transportation Theme

The Wheels on the Bus

The wheels on the bus go 'round and 'round, 'round and 'round,

'round and 'round.

The wheels on the bus go 'round and 'round,

All through the city streets

The people on the bus go up and down, up and down, up and down.

The people on the bus go up and down,

All through the city streets.

The wipers on the bus go swish, swish, swish, swish, swish, swish,

swish, swish, swish.

The wipers on the bus go swish, swish, swish,

All through the city streets.

The baby on the bus goes wah, wah, wah, [and so on].

The money on the bus goes clink, clink, clink, [and so on].

Follow-Up Activity

(1) This song lends itself to having the children create more verses, with accompanying noises and movements. Brainstorm other things that could happen on a bus and make up new verses.

(2) Transfer the verses onto large pieces of construction paper—one verse per page. Have the children pair up, and then have each set of partners illustrate a verse. (You might want to provide the outline of a bus.) Bind all the pages together to make a class book.

(3) Tape-record the children singing the song according to the class book. Place the book and the tape in the listening center for repeated listenings at free-choice time.

Pulgarcito

A Pulgarcito le invitaron (2×)

A dar un vue, vue, vuelo en un avión (2×)

¡Olé, olé, olé!

Y cuando estaban muy arriba (2×)

La gasoli-li-li se acabó (2×)

¡Olé, olé, olé!

Y Pulgarcito cayó al agua. (2×)

Y la balle-lle-llena lo comió. (2×)

¡Pobre Pulgarcito!

Follow-Up Activity

(1) Make a class mural of the three scenes from the song. Attach the verses under each section of the mural when complete. This is an excellent song to use for a Spanish as a second language lesson.

(2) Begin by brainstorming what should go in each section of the mural (e.g., Who invited Pulgarcito? Who is in the plane when it is way up high? What else would be in the water with the whale?)

(3) Divide the class into three groups. Give each child in the group a piece of newsprint to do his or her first draft of how the picture might look. Have the groups decide the best parts of each person's draft to include in the mural. (This is probably best done as a teacher- or aide-directed small-group activity for kindergarten and first grade.)

(4) Assign some children to work on the mural background, others to draw other items on colored construction paper to cut out and paste onto the background. Once the background and the other items are done, some time can be spent arranging the pieces on the background before final pasting is done.

(5) Review the song, using the completed mural.

Row, Row, Row Your Boat

Row, row, row your boat,

Gently down the stream.

Merrily, merrily, merrily, merrily,

Life is but a dream.

Ven, ven, ven acá,

Vamos a remar.

Rema que, rema que, rema que, rema que,

Vamos a remar.

El Barquito
(sung to the tune of "Eency Weency Spider")

Make a small blue sailboat. As you sing the song, have the children pass the boat around. As each child hands the boat to another, he or she states that child's name.

Azul es el cielo,

Azul es el mar,

Azul es el barquito

Que te voy a dar.

6 Assessment of Students

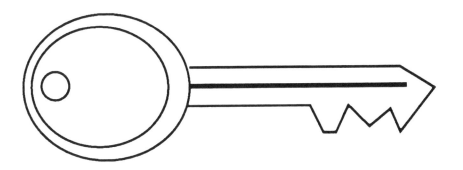

Assessment is a daily, ongoing process. The purpose of assessment is to find out both what your students know and how successful your teaching strategies have been. Assess what you plan to teach and what you think you've taught.

CHAPTER CONTENTS

ASSESSMENT OVERVIEW

Authentic assessments are built into the daily activities that students normally do. Any reading, writing, or math assignment provides information about what students know. It is important to collect that information and organize it in some way so that it can inform and guide your instructional decisions.

At the beginning of the year, especially in your first year of teaching, assessment can appear to be an overwhelming and impossible task. Finding the time to sit with an individual student for a period of time is difficult until classroom routines and procedures are established. Therefore, allow time, say two weeks, to get your classroom running smoothly before you try any individual assessment. This does not mean you won't be noting what your students know through observation, however.

It is also important to note that it usually takes a couple of weeks for K-1 students to feel comfortable in the school environment. Your assessment information will be more accurate when you have allowed this time for adjustment.

The important types of assessment information you collect on each student should include the following:

- samples of student work kept on a regular basis
- anecdotal records of your observations of students' involvement in learning activities
- individual assessments of the objectives of the curriculum

The following are some considerations about assessment:

- Attempt to assess only what will be useful to you for planning instruction, reporting to parents, and meeting district requirements.
- Plan a series of assessments—don't try to assess all the grade-level expectations at once. Expect to assess skills at least once a quarter in addition to the beginning of the year.
- Be familiar with the report card form, the parent conference form, and so on, to be sure you assess what you are expected to report.
- Try to do the assessments yourself. The process a student goes through in answering a question is often more instructive to you than the answer.
- In intermediate grades, tell the students what you will be looking for. Eventually, students can participate in the process of establishing assessment criteria.

Getting Started

Assessment Box: K-1

Prepare a box or Ziploc bag with all the materials you will need (e.g., pieces of construction paper of all the colors, shapes, counters, alphabet cards, sequence

Keys to the Classroom. © 1992 Corwin Press, Inc.

cards, numbers) to test the objectives you are required to report. Include in the box or bag the individual student record sheets you will be using to record the information. Having all the assessment materials organized in one spot will facilitate your being able to take advantage of spare moments to make assessments.

Anecdotal Records: K-6

Anecdotal records help you to focus on an individual student on a regular basis. You should plan on spending at least part of each day focusing on five to six children and writing your observations about what they are doing and saying, what they are interested in, and so on. If you observe five or six students a day, you will be observing each child once a week. Even if you observe only two or three students a day you will build up an impressive record over the year.

Observations can occur throughout the day. Think through your daily schedule to find a few minutes here and there that you could devote to observation.

Many times the task of keeping anecdotal records organized defeats teachers, and they give up on keeping them. Following are several ideas for how to organize the process. Choose one that you think fits your style.

- Make a notebook with dividers for all student. Carry binder paper on your clipboard. Put the child's name and the date at the top of the page. Record your observations. File the binder paper in the notebook at the end of the day. Or eliminate filing at the end of the day by carrying the binder with you and writing in it directly.

- Make a file box for index cards with a divider for each student. Each day, make a file card for each of the children you will be observing that day, including the date. Carry the file cards on a clipboard and make your notes on them. File the cards at the end of the day.

- Purchase peel-off address labels or Post-it Notes and carry these on your clipboard. Record your observations of each student on a separate label (remember to write the child's name and the date). At the end of the day, peel off the labels and stick them on the inside of the students' file folders.

Making anecdotal records a part of your daily routine will pay off when it comes to parent conference time as well as help you to understand the development of each student in your classroom.

Samples of Student Work

K-1. Plan to keep student work on a regular basis—once a week if possible. Be sure to date the work. Types of student work you might want to keep include self-portraits, writing samples, art projects, easel paintings, photocopies of journal entries, photocopies of pages read to you (with errors marked), and reproductions of math work. File the same entry for each student during any given week (e.g., file a self-portrait for everybody during Week 1, a writing sample during Week 2, a painting in Week 3, a math paper in Week 4, then start again with a self-portrait).

That way you will build up a compilation of similar types of samples that you can use to document growth or pinpoint areas of need.

2-6. Make two class folders for every student in your class (or have students make them the first day): a reading/writing folder and a math folder. These folders should be set up in a box file in alphabetical order. You will use these folders to begin to collect student work to use for assessment purposes and to document students' growth throughout the year. They will be useful for parent conferences, referrals, and report cards. Don't attempt to save every piece of student work. Students may decide at the end of the month their best two or three pieces, or you may choose a variety of kinds of work to save.

What goes into the student folders? Assignments you have coded SF (for student folder) in advance, any assessments, student or parent questionnaires, any significant pieces of student work that demonstrate growth or need—all are things you'll want to save.

Assessment is a critical part of your classroom. Unless you know your students' interests and abilities, you cannot meet their needs with an appropriate curriculum. Spending some time getting to know your students through observation, samples of work, and assessment of skills will give you more confidence in how much your students really do grow and change.

First-Month Assessments: K-1

The assessments you need to do during the first month of school with kindergartners and first graders are discussed below.

Observations to make for anecdotal records. The following are some ideas of what to look for to include in your anecdotal records. As your curriculum becomes more developed, you will add to this list, but this will help you get an idea of potential areas of need for specific students and allow you to look beyond academic knowledge into the social and physical development of your students.

- left-/right-handed
- attention to directions
- fine motor skills—cutting, holding a pencil, and so on
- enjoyment of learning activities
- intensity of involvement
- how student works—alone, with others, and so on
- independence
- types of choices student makes
- verbalizations—talking about what they're doing
- ability to complete tasks, both self-selected and teacher directed
- large motor skills
- interests

Assessment of skills. Below are listed some initial skills you may want to assess with individual students. Remember to prepare an assessment box/bag with the items you will need for the tests. Make individual student record sheets on which you can record the results. Leave space for comments on these sheets, as the ways students respond may be as important to note as the answers they give.

Remember, these are only initial assessments. You will expand these as the year progresses based on your grade-level expectations, reporting forms, and school policies.

Initial assessments in kindergarten include the following:

- color recognition
- shape recognition (square, circle, triangle, rectangle)
- rote counting
- one-to-one correspondence (counting objects)
- numeral recognition (0-10)
- recognition of own name when written

Initial assessments in first grade would include these areas:

- rote counting by ones and tens
- numeral recognition (0-20)
- one-to-one correspondence
- numeral writing (1-20)
- recitation of alphabet
- recognition of letters
- sound/symbol knowledge
- knowledge of difference between print and picture

ASSESSMENT FORMS

KINDERGARTEN/FIRST GRADE ASSESSMENT (SEPTEMBER-OCTOBER)

Student _____

Teacher _____

Assessment Dates _____

Language: Spanish _____ English _____ Other: _____

Can say the color: (X indicates student knows color)
    red/rojo_____
    yellow/amarillo_____
    black/negro_____
    white/blanco_____
    brown/café_____
    orange/anaranjado_____
    blue/azul_____
    purple/morado_____
    green/verde_____
    pink/rosita_____

Identifies by name: (X over shape indicates correct response)

Copies the following:

Rote counts 1-_____
1-1 correspondence 1-_____ (assess to 12 only)
Identifies numerals: (X over number indicates knowledge)
Kindergarten:

$$1 \quad 5 \quad 7 \quad 9 \quad 3$$
$$2 \quad 6 \quad 4 \quad 8 \quad 10$$

Add to first grade:

$$12 \quad 14 \quad 16 \quad 18$$
$$11 \quad 13 \quad 15 \quad 17$$
$$20 \quad 19$$

Writes numerals (0-9): (not an initial assessment for K; assess at a later date)
Circle one: Memory   Copied

Identifies own name from a group of seven names: Y   N

Writes first name (K)/last name (1):

_____

Given a familiar book with picture and print, demonstrates knowledge of the difference between picture and print: Y   N

Comments:_____

_____

When asked to read, demonstrates left-to-right tracking: Y   N

Comments:_____

_____

Using a familiar book, can retell the story in sequence: Y   N

Title:_____

Comments:_____

Keys to the Classroom. © 1992 Corwin Press, Inc.

ANECDOTAL RECORD FORM

Student Name _____

Date	Subject Area	Observations/Comments

CHECKLIST FOR ORAL READING

Assessment of oral reading should be done with students reading individually to you, either during silent reading time or in a private conference. If you do any writing as a student reads, it should be as unobtrusive as possible, and you should assure the student you have confidence in him or her and that you are just making notes to help you remember how well he or she reads. Information may be checked off on this form or listed later in an anecdotal record.

Reading Material _____ Date _____

Reading Fluency

[ ] very slowly, sounding out each word
[ ] word by word
[ ] quickly in phrases

Decoding Strategies for Unknown Words

[ ] looks for biggest known chunks (morphemes)
[ ] sounds out syllable by syllable
[ ] sounds out letter by letter

Note particular decoding errors, group errors.

Punctuation

[ ] ignores punctuation
[ ] stops for periods but shows no expression
[ ] expression appropriate to punctuation

General

[ ] reading material held too close or too far away (eye problem?)
[ ] uncomfortable, didn't like reading
[ ] doesn't respond appropriately to comprehension checks

How Challenging Is This Book for the Student?

[ ] very easy
[ ] enjoyable
[ ] challenging
[ ] frustrating

Keys to the Classroom. © 1992 Corwin Press, Inc.

OTHER READING/WRITING ASSESSMENTS

Five-Finger Test

This is a student self-assessment of independent reading level. Teach your students this quick method of determining their independent reading level early in the year:

(1) Choose a book.
(2) Choose a page and read silently to yourself.
(3) Place a finger on each unknown word on one page.
(4) When five fingers have been placed on a single page, you may decide that the book is too difficult for you to read alone.
(5) Choose another book and begin again.
(6) List in your reading record the book you decide to read.

Quick Sorts

Quick sorts are short, quick tests, usually for decoding and/or sight word reading ability. They are useful for a quick snapshot of where individual students are in these areas and will help you in grouping students to work on decoding and sight word skills. They should not be used to determine a child's reading placement for the rest of the year. Some examples of quick sorts are, for English reading, the San Diego Quick Assessment and the Slosson; for Spanish reading, the Santillana Quick Placement.

Assessing Student Writing

During the first month of school you will want to collect samples of several types of writing from students. These might include creative stories (from the Wiggly Line worksheet), letters (their letters to you), factual writing ("Who Lives at My House"), reflective writing (journals), and creating questions (various interview activities). Saving samples of each of these over time will allow you to see whether growth is taking place in both content and form. You won't have the time to record a detailed analysis of all the information that each piece can reveal, so you will need to scan for particular aspects that will inform your immediate instruction and help students focus on goals for themselves.

Monthly Writing Sample

On the first day of every month, have students write one page of their best writing. You can either have students save these pages in their writing folders or keep the pages posted on a bulletin board, with the current month's work stapled on top.

CHECKLIST FOR WRITING ASSESSMENT

This is a checklist for you to use in looking at student work and for notation on the anecdotal record form, not for red penciling student work. Use this list also to create student proofreading self-assessments. Do not look at every paper for every aspect of writing. Use the information you gather to plan what lessons you will teach. Is it something the whole class will need or just a small group?

Content of Writing, Narrative (any fictional story)

[ ] Is there a sequence—beginning, middle, and end?
[ ] Does a plot develop—problem, response, action, outcome? Is it believable, logical, exciting?
[ ] Are there interesting characters? (Good description?)
[ ] Does the setting add to the story? (Good description?)

Content of Writing, Expository (any nonfiction explanatory writing)

[ ] What kind of organizational structure was used in prewriting? (Matrix, hierarchy, web, outline, list?)
[ ] Are there supporting facts?
[ ] Are there smooth transitions between statements, paragraphs?

Mechanics of Writing

[ ] Was appropriate form used? (Paragraphs, letter format, title?)
[ ] Are there trends in the kinds of grammar errors made?
[ ] What kinds of punctuation/capitalization errors occurred?
[ ] How is the sentence structure? Is there space between words?

Spelling

[ ] Are there phonetic problems, families of words?
[ ] What are the most common misspellings?
[ ] Are misspellings due to oral/aural language problems?
[ ] Is your spelling program covering the errors?

(Spelling programs are a question you'll need to deal with at your school site. If you don't feel the current program is meeting your students' needs, you will need to be

Keys to the Classroom. © *1992 Corwin Press, Inc.*

able to articulate an alternative to parents and administration clearly before changing your approach.)

Penmanship

[ ] Are there problems with basic letter formation?
[ ] Is motor coordination a problem?
[ ] Is neatness a problem? Is there a difference between a draft and a published copy?
[ ] What could the student do to improve his or her penmanship?

STUDENT SELF-ASSESSMENT

An important routine to establish with students is that of proofreading their own and each others' work. A short, simple checklist to reinforce skills taught or to focus on a student's individual needs is very helpful. Ask them to look for no more than three aspects of their writing. Assign a standard check sheet or have students create their own from the Checklist for Writing Assessment.

Sample Proofreading Checklist

[ ] Did I indent the paragraphs?

[ ] Did I give details to support my opinions?

[ ] Did I capitalize all proper names and beginning of sentences?

[ ] ¿Están endentados mis párrafos?

[ ] ¿Dí suficientes detalles para arirmar mis opiniones?

[ ] ¿Usé letras mayúsculas al principio de mis oraciones y en nombres propios?

WRITING PROCESS OBSERVATION CHECKLIST

When students are working on writing, you will find your class in various stages of the writing process. You will want a simple, efficient way to keep track of what students are working on and where their strengths and needs are. This checklist is designed for assessment of each of the stages of the writing process. As students work, walk around with the Weekly Writing Process Observation Form and make comments as to their progress in the particular stages they are working on in the writing process. If you have 30 students you will need to comment on only 6 each day to cover the entire class by the end of a week. This will leave you plenty of time for individual conferences and other supportive work.

In all stages of the process it may be useful to note whether students are on task, who they are working with, and what their attitudes seem to be about what they are doing, as well as any areas that you work on with a student. Here are some suggestions to think about at each stage:

Prewriting: Does the student demonstrate organizational skills, brainstorming, mind mapping, outlining, note taking? Does the student have difficulty in this phase? What might the obstacles be?
Drafting: Does the student write fluently? (Note number of words or lines written.) Does spelling get in the way? Is the student comfortable inventing spelling? (Note topics the student writes on.)
Revision: See the content sections of the Checklist for Writing Assessment for possible areas of revision. What motivates the student to revise? Does the student find his or her own areas of weakness? Whose feedback does the student value?
Editing: See the mechanics section of the Checklist for Writing Assessment. Does the student become overwhelmed by mechanical problems?
Publishing: What form does the student choose for publishing? (Note how long this process takes and the student's attitude toward publishing the work.)

Remember, the point is not to write copious notes on students, but simply to jot down quick observations that will indicate to you where students are and what they were doing on the day that you checked in with them. The following is an example of how the observation form can be used (codes are explained on the following page).

Week of _Feb. 17, 1992_

Names of Students	Topic/Story		Comments (stage appropriate)
Juan Garcia	fish	D	3 pages / check setting
Katy Davis	unicorns	D	slow start

WEEKLY WRITING PROCESS OBSERVATION FORM

Codes for stages: PW = prewriting, D = drafting, R = revising, E = editing,
P = publishing
Week of _____

Names of Students	Topic/Story	Comments (stage appropriate)

CLASSROOM BEHAVIOR DURING WORK TIME

Codes for behaviors: OT = on task, DO = distracting others, QD = quiet but distracted, LO = leading others, WC = working cooperatively, I = interested, B = bored, F = frustrated
Your own codes:
Week of _____

Names	Independent Work Time	Cooperative Groups	Transitions

READING COMPREHENSION ASSESSMENT

Find three different consecutive levels of basal texts and copy a selection from each. Assess your students individually for reading comprehension. The information from these assessments will help you decide the literature level to provide your students. The quality of responses will help you determine the thought processes of the students and their depth of understanding. In your anecdotal log, note the use of complete sentences, details, and elaboration.

Give the following written instructions to students:

Complete the following when you have read the story:
 Write six facts from the story.
 From what you read in the story, describe what the main character looked like.
 Tell in your own words what the story is about.
 Explain why the story has the title that it does.
 Choose a picture in the story. Write what happened BEFORE that picture and write what happened AFTER the picture.

Completa la siguiente cuando ha leido el cuento.
 Escribe seis hechos que pasaron en el cuento.
 Dá una descripción personal del personaje principal del cuento.
 En tus propias palabras cuenta de que se trata el cuento.
 Explica por qué el cuento tiene ese título.
 Escoge una ilustración del cuento. Escribe qué pasó ANTES de esa ilustración y escribe lo qué pasó DESPUÉS de esa ilustración.

MATH ASSESSMENT

Computational Skills

To assess your class in computation skills quickly, create worksheets that start with very easy skills and become increasingly more difficult (every math book has lots of these). This will allow all students to work successfully through some of the test. Explain that you don't expect students to finish all the problems. Provide enough problems and limit time such that the quickest students don't quite finish. This way, everyone will experience the same sense of being challenged. No one will feel he or she was the only one who couldn't finish.

Assess your students in addition facts (Do they know simple facts in their heads? Can they carry?), subtraction facts (Can they borrow?), multiplication tables, division (basic, long division), decimals, and place value. Do they understand basic math vocabulary?

A quick check in addition might look like the following:

$$
\begin{array}{cccccc}
3 & 7 & 5 & 12 & 56 & 34 \\
+6 & +9 & +5 & +23 & +11 & +65
\end{array}
$$

$$
\begin{array}{cccc}
47 & 58 & 186 & 134 \\
+26 & +93 & +123 & +\ 27
\end{array}
$$

$$
\begin{array}{cccc}
4583 & 5261 & \$38.29 & \$62.94 \\
+3754 & +\ 3452 & +19.98 & 24.83
\end{array}
$$

Problem Solving

Mary spent $1.49 on pencils and $3.57 on a binder. How much did she spend all together on her school supplies?

7 Parent Communications: Sample Letters in English and Spanish

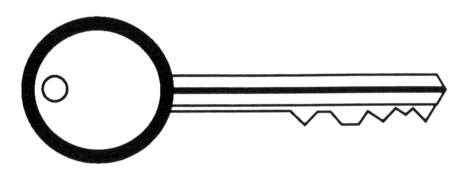

Positive communications with your students' parents will strengthen your classroom in many ways.

Dear Parents:

It's hard to believe that summer is almost over, but here we are, about to embark on what I hope will be an exciting and productive year for your child. I am anxious to see that we have a smooth beginning. In order to ensure that, I am listing a few of the ways you can help _____ adjust to his/her first day of school.

(1) In order to alleviate your child's first-day fears, talk to him/her about what to anticipate; that school will be a fun, busy learning time.

(2) Arrive early (anytime after ____), to room ____, next ____, so that I can have an opportunity to greet you.

(3) Once the first school bell rings, I will ask all parents to leave the room. This will make it easier for the children and me to bond and will facilitate your child's adaptation to school. I DO want parents in the classroom later on, because I strongly believe that your involvement is a key to your child's success. I will be making a strong plea for parent volunteers in a few weeks.

(4) If your child rides the bus home that first day, assure him/her that you will be waiting at the bus stop when he/she arrives. I will have a list of the bus stops posted in the classroom.

I am looking forward to meeting you!

Estimados Padres:

Parece méntira que ya casi se terminó el verano, pero así es y estamos a punto de embarcarnos en un nuevo año escolar. Espero que sea un año productivo y estimulante para su hijo/a. Mi mayor deseo es que el principio de este año sea tranquilo. Para asegurarnos de que _____ se adapte fácilmente en su primer día de escuela, les sugerio lo siguiente:

(1) Para reducir a la ansiedad del primer día de escuela, platique con el o ella tocante a lo que puedan anticipar: Que ir a la escuela es divertido y que van a estar muy ocupados aprendiendo muchas cosas nuevas.

(2) Llegue temprano (despues de las _____), al salón _____ el próximo _____, para yo tener la oportunidad de darles la bienvenida.

(3) En cuanto suene la campana, yo les voy a pedir a todos los padres que se retiren del salón. Así el vínculo entre los niños y la maestra se establese y es más fácil la adaptación de los niños a la escuela. Mas adelante SI voy a querer la presencia de los padres en el salón porqué yo creo que la clave del éxito escolar es su participación. En unas semanas voy a pedirles a los padres vigorozamente que sirvan de voluntarios en el salón.

(4) Si sus hijos se van en el camión el primer día, asegúreles a ellos que Uds. van a estar esperándolos en la parada cuando lleguen. En el salón voy a tener una lista de las paradas del camión.

¡Estoy anticipando el gusto de conocerlos!

Donation List

We are also in need of some materials for our art center. If you have any of these items to donate, we would greatly appreciate it.

    fabric scraps
    paper towel rolls
    colored pencils
    buttons
    shells
    seeds, beans, peas
    yarn
    string
    ribbon
    different shapes of macaroni
    Popsicle sticks
    needles and thread
    felt pieces
    small wood scraps
    squares of cardboard
    felt-tip markers (fat and thin)
    toothpicks
    straws
    bottle caps
    spools
    measuring cups and spoons
    sponges (old)
    old shirts

Lista de Donativo

También necesitamos algunos materiales para el centro del arte. Si ustedes tienen algunos de estos materiales disponibles para donarlos, se lo agradeceremos mucho.

        pedazos de tela
        rollos de toallas de papel
        lápices de colores
        botones
        conchas de mar
        semillas, frijoles, chícharos
        estambre
        cordón
        listón
        macarrón de diferentes figuras
        palitos de paletas
        hilos y agujas
        tela de fieltro
        pedazos de madera chicos
        cuadros de cartón
        plumones (gordos y delgados)
        palillos
        popotes
        corcholatas de botella
        carretes de hilo vacíos
        tazas y cucharas para medir
        esponjas (viejas)
        camisas viejas

Dear Parents:

Our class has voted to have a daily snack at approximately____.
It was decided that each child who wanted to participate would
bring a "healthy snack" about once a month. I will send home a
note announcing your child's day to bring a snack. Some suggestions are crackers, cheese, fruit, baked goods, nuts, raisins,
granola, popcorn, carrots, celery, or other vegetables. There
are generally __ people in the classroom.

Your support in this program is appreciated. If you would prefer that your child not participate, just send a note or call.
If you have any other questions or concerns, feel free to get
in touch.

Thank you,

Your child is scheduled to bring a snack on _____.

Estimados Padres:

Nuestra clase ha votado a favor de tener un bocadillo a las ___ aproximadamente. Se decidió que cada niño o niña que quiera participar traiga "un bocadillo nutritivo" una vez al mes. Voy a mandar un recado indicándoles el día que les va a tocar traerlo a su niño o niña. Algunos de los bocadillos que sug-erimos son galletas, queso, fruta, postres horneados en casa, nueces, pasas, granola, palomitas de maíz, zanahorias, apio, o alguna otra verdura. Por lo general hay __ personas en la clase.

Su apoyo en éste programa será muy apreciado. Si prefieren que su hijo o hija no participe en éste programa, nada más manden un recado o comuníquese por teléfono conmigo. Si tienen Uds. alguna pregunta o algo les preocupa comuníquese conmigo con confianza.

Gracias,

El día que le toca a su hijo/a traer bocadillo es _____.

Dear Parents:

I realize you are busy with your jobs, lives, and families. If time permits, I'd love your help in the classroom. Please take a few minutes to look over the list below to see if you can help.

[ ] Typing. Commitment: twice during the year.

[ ] Handle book club orders. Commitment: once a month or every 6-10 weeks.

[ ] Working with individuals or a small group with math. Commitment: once a month to several times a week.

[ ] Listening to children read aloud, any day except Friday. Commitment: once a month to several times a week.

[ ] Leading a literature group (leading a discussion of a novel with a small group of children), any day except Friday, 8:45-9:40. Commitment: once or twice a week for the duration of the book.

[ ] Room parent (general support and primarily help with the carnival—the children pretty well organize their own parties).

[ ] Talking to the class or small group about your career. Commitment: one time, to be arranged after December.

[ ] Driving on field trips (you must have insurance and seat belts).

[ ] Cooking with small groups of students.

[ ] Reading to the class once a week, Monday-Thursday, 1:00-1:30.

[ ] Anything I missed?

If you have any questions or need more information before signing your time away, please call me at _____.

Thank you,

_____   _____
Parent's name   Parent's telephone

Estimados Padres:

Comprendo que están muy ocupados con su trabajo, vidas, y demás responsabilidades en casa. Si tienen el tiempo, me encantaría tener su ayuda en mi salón de clases. Por favor tome unos minutos para revisar la lista que sigue a ver si pueden ayudarme.

[ ] Escribir en máquina. Obligaciónes: solamente dos veces al año.

[ ] Hacerse cargo de tomar las ordenes del Libro del Mes. Obligaciones: una vez al mes o, cada 6-10 semanas.

[ ] Dirigir un grupo de literatura (dirigiendo una discusión de una novela con un grupo de niños), cualquier día excepto viernes, 8:45-9:40. Obligación: una o dos veces a la semana o hasta que se termine el libro.

[ ] Madre o padre de salón (apoyo en general principalmente con el carnaval—los estudiantes más o menos organizan sus fiestas en la clase por si mismos).

[ ] Visitar el salón y hablar acerca de su ocupación. Obligación: una vez nada más y los arreglos se harán después de diciembre.

[ ] Ayudar a transportar estudiantes en las excursiones de la escuela (se debe tener aseguranza en el carro y cinturones de seguridad).

[ ] Cocinar con un grupo pequeño de estudiantes.

[ ] Leer a la clase en voz alta una vez por semana, lunes-jueves, 1:00-1:30.

[ ] ¿Algo más que se me olvidó mencionar?
   .

Si tienen alguna pregunta o necesitan información adicional antes de comprometer su tiempo, por favor llame al _____.

Gracias,

_____   _____
    Nombre de padres   Teléfono de padres

Keys to the Classroom. © 1992 Corwin Press, Inc.

Dear Parents:

This is a note about homework. Your child will have homework
every night except Fridays. The intent of the homework is
threefold: (1) it helps to build responsibility in the children, as they are responsible for the completion and the transportation of the work; (2) it gives the students an
opportunity to practice skills taught in the class; and (3) it
gives you a chance to become involved with your child's class
work.

Children are most successful with homework if the time and
place for work are consistent. A quiet desk to work at and a
regular time, such as right before or after dinner, seem to be
the most beneficial.

Below is a copy of your student's homework schedule. Please
keep it as a reminder.

Thank you,

HOMEWORK SCHEDULE

    MONDAY:
    TUESDAY:
    WEDNESDAY:
    THURSDAY:

Estimados Padres:

Esta nota es referente a la assignación de tareas. Su hijo/a tendrá tarea todos los días excepto el viernes. La tarea sirve tres propósitos: (1) ayuda al estudiante a ser responsable hacer el trabajo, completarlo y transportarlo; (2) le dá la oportunidad al estudiante de practicar la habilidad adquirida en la clase; y (3) les dá a Uds. la oportunidad de envolverse con el trabajo escolar de su estudiante.

Los estudiantes tienen más éxito cuando el lugar y el tiempo para hacer la tarea es el mismo. Escoja un lugar determinado y conveniente para que su hijo/a haga su tarea, guarde sus papeles y recuérdele traerlo a la clase al día siguiente.

En seguida está la lista de los días de tarea. Por favor guárdela como un recordatorio.

Gracias,

LISTA DE LOS DÍAS DE TAREA

    LUNES:
    MARTES:
    MIERCOLES:
    JUEVES:

Dear Parents:

This year we are working on the writing process. This process involves these main steps:

(1) *Prewriting:* thinking, getting started
(2) *Rough drafts:* writing ideas down
(3) *Revising:* making the words clearer, the content more interesting; making additions, deletions, changes
(4) *Editing and proofreading:* correcting spelling, grammar, punctuation
(5) *Publishing:* completing the finished work, final copy

Not all writing will go through all five steps. Some may go through only step two or three. In that case, a paper that comes home would be stamped "unedited," which means it was checked for content only.

If your child asks you to read a piece of his/her writing, ask if you are reading it (1) for enjoyment (sharing), (2) for comments about the content (Is it understandable?), or (3) for editing (correcting spelling, punctuation, grammar). Your responses would vary according to the purpose. Here are some suggested comments or questions:

(1) *Enjoyment:* Wonderful! I really liked this part. . . . How did you think of this idea?
(2) *Content:* I'm not sure what you mean here. This part is not very clear. Read it out loud to me. It doesn't feel finished—are you going to write more?
(3) *Editing:* Is it okay if I write on your paper? Should I use a pen or pencil?

It is my hope that this will help you and your child enjoy writing and the written word together.

Sincerely,

Estimados Padres:

Estamos trabajando en el proceso de escritura éste año. Éste proceso consiste de los siguientes pasos principales:

(1) *Antes de escribir:* pensar, prepararce para empezar

(2) *Escribir:* escribir ideas en papel

(3) *Revisar:* hacer las palabras más claras, el contenido mas interesante; agregar, tachar, hacer cambios

(4) *Repaso y corrección de pruebas:* corregir ortografía, gramática, y puntuación

(5) *Publicación:* terminar el trabajo completo, copiar en limpio

No todos los trabajos de escritura van a seguir los cinco pasos. Algunos trabajos nadamás van a seguir los pasos dos o tres. En ese caso los papeles que los alumnos lleven a casa van tener un sello que dirá "no corregído" lo cual quiere decir que solamente el contenido ha sido revisado, no la ortografía, gramática o puntuación.

Si su niño o niña le pide a ustedes que lean algo que ellos han escrito, pregúntele para qué propósito: (1) por el gusto de compartir, (2) para comentarios sobre el contenido (¿Se entiende?), o (3) para hacer correcciónes de ortógrafia, puntuación, gramática. Sus respuestas tienen que ser diferentes según el propósito de la pregunta. Los siguientes comentarios o preguntas son recomendables.

(1) *Por el gusto de compartir:* Magnífico, de verás me gusta ésta parte. . . . ¿Cómo se te ocurrió esa idea?

(2) *Contenido:* No estoy muy seguro/a de lo que quieres decir aquí. Esta parte no está muy clara. Lee esa parte en voz alta. Parece que la idea no ésta completa—¿vas a escribir más?

(3) *Correcciónes:* ¿Puedo escribir en tu papel? ¿Debo usar pluma o lápiz?

Con la esperanza de que la presente ayude a ustedes y a su hijo/a gozar la escritura y de la palabra escrita.

Sinceramente,

Keys to the Classroom. © *1992 Corwin Press, Inc.*

8 Resources

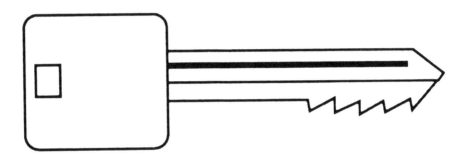

The books in the following bibliography are good sources of activities as are those mentioned in the previous chapters.

CHAPTER CONTENTS

BIBLIOGRAPHY
FOR TEACHERS

Conflict Resolution

Kreidler, W. J. (1984). *Creative conflict resolution: More than 200 ideas for keeping peace in the classroom.* Santa Monica, CA: Goodyear.

Literacy

Hancock, J., & Hill, S. (1987). *Literature-based reading programs at work.* Portsmouth, NH: Heinemann.

Johnson, T. D., & Louis, D. R. (n.d.). *Bringing it all together.* Portsmouth, NH: Heinemann.

Johnson, T. D., & Louis, D. R. (1987). *Literacy through literature.* Portsmouth, NH: Heinemann.

McCormick-Calkins, L. (1986). *The art of teaching writing.* Portsmouth, NH: Heinemann.

McCraken, R., & McCraken, M. (1978). *Reading, writing and language.* Winnipeg: Peguis.

McCraken, R., & McCraken, M. (1987). *Reading is only the tiger's tail.* Winnipeg: Peguis.

McCraken, R., & McCraken, M. (1987). *Stories, songs and poetry to teach reading and writing.* Winnipeg: Peguis.

Routman, R. (n.d.). *Invitations.* Portsmouth, NH: Heinemann.

Routman, R. (1988). *Transitions from literature to literacy.* Portsmouth, NH: Heinemann.

Math

Baratta-Lorton, M. (1976). *Mathematics their way.* Menlo Park, CA: Addison-Wesley.

Baratta-Lorton, R. (1977). *Mathematics: A way of thinking.* Menlo Park, CA: Addison-Wesley.

Burns, M. (1987). *A collection of math lessons from grades 1 through 3.* New Rochelle, NY: Cuisenaire.

Burns, M. (1987). *A collection of math lessons from grades 3 through 6.* New Rochelle, NY: Cuisenaire.

Burns, M. (n.d.). *The good time math event book.* Concord, CA: Creative Publications.

Cook, M. (1983). *Mathematics problems of the day.* Concord, CA: Creative Publications.

Cossey, R., Stenmark, J. K., & Thompson, V. (1986). *Family math.* Berkeley: Lawrence Hall of Science/University of California Regents.

Day, L., Langhort, C., & Skolnick, J. (n.d.). *How to encourage girls in math and science.* Englewood Cliffs, NJ: Prentice-Hall.

Downie, D., Slesnick, T., & Stenmark, J. K. (1981). *Math for girls and other problem solvers.* Berkeley: Lawrence Hall of Science/University of California Regents.

Physical Education

Fluegelman, A. (1976). *The new games book*. Garden City, NY: Dolphin/Doubleday.
Harris, F. (1990). *Games*. Belmont, CA: Fearon Teacher Aids/Simon & Schuster.
Kamiya, A. (1985). *Elementary teacher's handbook of indoor & outdoor games*. Englewood Cliffs, NJ: Prentice-Hall.
Larnes, C. (1983). *Awesome elementary school physical education activities*. (Available from the author at 3949 Linus Way, Carmichael, CA.)

Team Building/Self-Esteem

Gibbs, J. (1978). *Tribes*. Berkeley, CA: Center Source.
Howe, L., Kershenbaum, H., & Simon, S. B. (n.d.). *Values clarification*. Denver, CO: Hart.
Kagan, S. (1988). *Cooperative learning resources for teachers*. Laguna Niguel, CA.
White, E. (1980). *Nourishing the seeds of self esteem*. Capitola, CA: Whitenwife.

READ-ALOUDS, K-6, IN ENGLISH AND SPANISH

English

Book titles in this list that are followed by asterisks are also available in Spanish.

Kindergarten

Benjamin's 365 Birthdays, Judi Barrett
Caps for Sale, Esphyr Slobodkira
Corduroy,* Don Freeman
Goodnight Moon, Margaret Brown
Ira Sleeps Over, Bernard Waber
Rosie's Walk, Pat Hutchins
The Snowy Day, Ezra Jack Keats

First Grade

The Carrot Seed, Ruth Krauss
Curious George,* H. A. Rey
Noisey Nora, Rosemary Wells
Rhymes About Us, Marchette Chute
Stone Soup, Marcia Brown
Tiki, Tiki Tembo, Arlene Mosel

Second Grade

A Birthday for Frances, Russell Hoban
The Carp in the Bathtub, Barbara Cohen

*Frog and Toad Are Friends,** Arnold Lobel
The Island of the Skog, Steven Kellog
Miss Nelson Is Missing, Harry Allard
Stone Soup, Marcia Brown
*Sylvester and the Magic Pebble,** William Steig

Third Grade

A Bear Called Paddington, Michael Bond
The Borrowers, Mary Norton
*Charlotte's Web,** E. B. White
The Great Brain, Mary Norton
The Lion, the Witch, and the Wardrobe, C. S. Lewis
Miss Rumphius, Barbara Cooney
The Mouse and the Motorcycle, Beverly Cleary
Soup on Fire, Robert Newton Peck
Strega Nona, Tomi DePaola
Stuart Little, E. B. White

Fourth Grade

From the Mixed-Up Files of Mrs. Basil E. Frankweiler, E. L. Koningsburg
The Girl Who Cried Flowers, Jane Yolen
*Island of the Blue Dolphins,** Scott O'Dell
*James and the Giant Peach,** Roald Dahl
Mrs. Frisby and the Rats of NIMH, Robert C. O'Brien
*Ramona the Pest,** Beverly Cleary
*Tales of a Fourth Grade Nothing,** Judy Blume

Fifth Grade

The Incredible Journey, Sheila Burnford
Owls in the Family, Farley Mowat
Philip Hall Likes Me, I Reckon . . . Maybe, Bette Greene
The Pinballs, Betsy Byars
Sign of the Beaver, Elizabeth Speare
Sing Down the Moon, Scott O'Dell
Summer of the Swans, Betsy Byars

Sixth Grade

*Bridge to Terabithia,** Katherine Paterson
Call It Courage, Armstrong Sperry
Ring of Endless Light, Madeleine L'Engle
Roll of Thunder, Hear My Cry, Mildred Taylor
Sounder, Will Armstrong

Spanish

Kindergarten

Corduroy, Don Freeman
Donde Viven Los Monstruos, Maurice Sendak
Historía de la Pollita, Mary DeBall Kwitz
El Oso Más Elegante, Mary Blocksma
El Primer Día de Escuela, Helen Oxenbury
Tortillitas Para Mamá, Griego y Bucks

Primero

¿Eres tú Mi Mamá?, P. D. Eastman
El Poni, el Oso, y el Manzano, Sigrid Heuck
Jorge, el Curioso, H. A. Rey
Angus y el Gato, Marjorie Flack
Nadarín, Leo Lionni

Segundo

Buenos Días, Querida Ballena, Achim Broger
Osito, Else H. Minarik
Sapo y Sepo, Inseparables, Arnold Lobel
Sylvestre y la Piedra Mágica, William Steig
El Viejo Reloj, Fernando Alonso

Tercero

Aventuras de Connie y Diego, María Garcia
Hansel y Gretel, los Hermanos Grimm
El Patito Feo, Hans Christian Andersen
Ramona la Chinche, Beverly Cleary

Cuarto

La Bruja que Quiso Matar al Sol, Ricardo Alcantara
La Calle es Libre, Kurasa
Platero y Yo, Juan Ramón Jimenez
Telarañas de Charlotte, E. B. White